STRATEGIES FOR PLAYBUILDING

STRATEGIES FOR PLAYBUILDING

Helping Groups Translate Issues into Theatre

WILL WEIGLER

HEINEMANN
Portsmouth, NH

Heinemann
361 Hanover Street
Portsmouth, NH 03801–3912
www.heinemann.com

Offices and agents throughout the world

The author and publisher wish to thank those who have generously given permission to reprint borrowed material:

The cartoon on page 75 is reprinted with the kind permission of Magi Wechsler, the artist. The cartoon originally appeared in the Neue Zürcher Zeitung (NZZ) 49/70.

"Independence" from *Changing Directions*, produced by Young Actors' Forum, 1989 and "Does It Have to Come to This?" and "Barbara Johns" from *Turn Loose the Voices*, produced by Young Actors' Forum, 1991, are reprinted by permission.

The text from the "Joseph Cruthers Public Service Announcement" is reprinted with the gracious permission of the Urban Alliance on Race Relations, Toronto, Ontario.

The excerpt from *Road* by Jim Cartwright, published in 1986, is reprinted by permission of Methuen Drama.

Library of Congress Cataloging-in-Publication Data
Weigler, Will.
Strategies for playbuilding : helping groups translate issues into theatre / Will Weigler.
p. cm.
ISBN 0-325-00340-8 (alk. paper)
1. Improvisation (Acting). 2. Playwriting. I. Title.

PN2071.I5 W45 2001
792′.028—dc21 00–050565

Editor: Lisa A. Barnett
Production: Sonja S. Chapman
Cover design: Joni Doherty
Manufacturing: Deanna Richardson

Printed in the United States of America
21 20 19 18 GP 4 5 6 7

For Eva Lee

CONTENTS

FOREWORD

For most people in our culture, theatre is entertainment. Young people's exposure to theatre is minimal and casual. We do not have an educated or sensitive young audience for plays though exposure to TV and movies are pervasive and often obsessive. Yet, theatre can be a vehicle for the development of ideas, the articulation and understanding of feelings, and the development of political and social conscience. Opportunity and experience with playbuilding and performance is all too lacking for the young, and yet, it is one of the most powerful ways in which awareness, sensitivity, and community can be developed.

Will Weigler's book is an introduction to the way in which making plays can help young people translate important issues that puzzle them, or prey on their minds into articulate dramatic statements. The plays produced through the processes illustrated and demonstrated in this book are practical and from my experience, effective. They provide young people occasions to become articulate about their experiences through dramatic play, and performance with others.

The book is equally useful to professionals in the theatre, and others who are doing theatre with young people. They all can benefit from the exercises, themes, improvisations, and production suggestions provided. It is particularly useful for people who want to do theatre with youngsters, who understand the expressive power of drama and comedy, and who need a way to jump in and be guided through their first efforts in making and performing plays with young people.

Having done theatre and play making with the young for years, I had developed old habits of working. This book provides many new ideas and themes and in particular, ways of transforming serious social, personal, and political issues into plays, and I certainly hope to use them over the next years.

—Herbert Kohl

ACKNOWLEDGMENTS

When I was a teenage actor in Portland, Oregon, there were three theatre directors who continually showed me the same respect they gave to adult actors. Even though I was usually the youngest one in the class or the cast, they made me feel that my contribution—what I had to offer—was important. Their confidence in me had a tremendous impact on my life, my love of theatre, and my dedication to helping kids now that I'm an adult. Thank you, Howard Thoresen, Steve Smith, and Jack Featheringill.

Thanks to Phyllis Gorfain at Oberlin College for introducing me to new ideas and challenging me to see with fresh eyes what I thought I already knew.

Thanks to all my family, friends, and colleagues who shared their thoughts and read the manuscript as it evolved, marking each draft with circles, arrows, and exclamation points to show what they liked and how the rest of it could be improved. Thanks especially to TR for her lifelong support and exhaustive attention to detail.

Thanks to my hardworking Production Editor, Sonja Chapman and to Lisa A. Barnett for her wit and stewardship.

I will always be indebted to the wonderfully talented young actors I've been privileged to work with over the years. They really have taught me what I know through their willingness to try out ideas, watch the experiments fail, and then jump right up and try out more ideas. I am constantly astonished by the brilliance of their artistry. I couldn't have written this book without them.

And finally, thank you to Eva Lee Sargent, for all the adventure, passion, and laughter.

INTRODUCTION

This book offers the reader a practical, step-by-step approach to helping a group of young people collaboratively investigate the issues that concern them and turn their perceptions into a script, song lyrics, or choreography. It provides a series of exercises and techniques that suggest *what to do* and *why*, from the first meeting through rehearsals to performances. The process enables participants of different ages, abilities, and experiences to contribute equally. It promotes ownership, so that the script is a result of the cast's own analytic and creative work, not something written for the actors by an adult. It also emphasizes high quality, so that an audience of peers or adults will take the performers seriously and give genuine consideration to their ideas. The creative challenge of turning discussion and research into exciting theatre is a fun and dynamic way to involve young people in the issues facing their community. Performing their work gives them a powerful means to share their views with others.

Even when used on a smaller scale, for example, by collectively writing songs for performance within a classroom, these techniques can engage young people and give them focus and a sense of accomplishment. The methodology is not designed just for kids. Adults looking for ways to examine and animate the dialogues about issues facing their community will find in these exercises an exciting alternative to more conventional discussion formats.

Although most of this book is devoted to strategies for developing a script, there are also sections on other aspects of producing a show, such as directing, rehearsing, and developing the participants' performance skills.

The techniques in this book were developed out of frustration. As a director of young people's theatre, I've worked with kids who were brimming with conviction and passion about contemporary social issues, but it was always a struggle for me to help them translate their insights into a script that was artistically engaging. Their writing and improvisation about socially relevant issues generally led to talky scenes that didn't hold interest dramatically. It was difficult to discourage their tendency to play out scenes and characters drawn straight from television and film or to create moralistic tales based on what they felt the audience should be taught.

To overcome these challenges, I tried reconsidering their role in the process. I started asking them to think of themselves not as *actors* creating individual characters, but as *artists* looking for ways to communicate their perceptions.

I asked them to tell stories about actual events in their experiences related to our chosen topic. Rather than dramatize the stories as actors, they *unpacked* them: they together identified the most vivid, compelling elements in each story, pointing out the single phrases, gestures, sounds, and images that, for them, reflected the essence of the event. It was an exciting exercise that drew upon their natural abilities as social observers. The elements they pulled out were inherently theatrical: these were the turning points, the subtle and glaring moments that defined the very nature of the relationships in the stories. They told more stories and unpacked those. By stripping away the extraneous details of half a dozen different stories on the same basic topic, they found it surprisingly easy to identify patterns in what people had done or said. They began to appreciate the potential for incorporating these elements into one scene or song or dance that would capture the sense of what people do in situations like the ones they were examining.

But it wasn't enough to identify evocative elements or patterns of behavior. The performers also had to be able to present what they were learning in a dramatic form on stage. So, as artists, they began to experiment with found (commonplace) objects, props, and musical instruments, using them as tools to stage visual and aural metaphors that most elegantly and powerfully characterized their observations. How different were the results of this work compared to their earlier work! Instead of just inventing dialogue, the actors were fiercely searching for the most effective and theatrically exciting ways to show how they saw the world. As the exercises progressed, the actors became adept at bringing together all the different elements—text, movement, props, and music—to collaboratively orchestrate a piece of theatre that would express the insights they were discovering.

Ultimately, by approaching script development in this way, cast members were able to exercise substantial control over creating theatre that communicated their collective vision. As far as I was concerned, it stood in stark contrast to the much more commonly used character-based method for creating a script through group improvisation. In that tradition, the actors determine their circumstances (where they are, what's happened), choose characters, and decide what each character wants (motivations). Then, in character, the actors play out what they want while something or someone tries to prevent them from getting it (the dramatic conflict). The results are recorded, written up, and refined into a script.

I often found that the actors developing material in this way were severely limited in what they could accomplish. During the improvisation, individual actors had very little control over shaping the whole script. The direction the scene took was generally dictated by the most forceful actor involved. Those with less experience, or less facility with language, were left behind. As the improvisation progressed, it became very easy for the actors to slip into clichés, to sacrifice truthfulness for dramatic action, and, consciously or not, to steer the scene toward making moral judgments about the characters. Aware that the purpose of the play was to convey a point of view, the actors would tend to predetermine the meaning and then make their characters illustrate that meaning. The good girl did the right thing and was rewarded; the bad boy went down the wrong path and met with trouble.

This was especially true when the cast dealt with social issues. It takes an extremely disciplined actor to ignore all the stereotyped images bombarding us each day through advertising, television, and film. These images shape our preconceptions about people and situations. A character-oriented improvisation model encouraged the little playwright in each actor's head to spin out tales drawn from those preconceptions. The tales the actors wove often followed the lead of television and film, where dramatic action frequently takes precedent over truthfulness and where moral judgments about characters are the stock in trade.

Even when actors created autobiographical work, written or improvised, that authentically reproduced what they felt at a given time in their lives, they were seldom challenged to think critically about the experience. At best, members of the audience seeing their work could be touched by the recognition that another's experience was like their own. The process didn't take advantage of the actors' potential for putting an experience in context, understanding it, and consciously shaping a piece of theatre that would communicate insight about it.

This is, perhaps, the most significant thing that separates the script development process in this book from other approaches. By telling stories about related situations, paying attention to the phrases, gestures, sounds, and images in each one, and looking for consistent patterns, the actors build their sense of what happens while they are gathering evocative, dramatic material to help them illustrate it. They experiment to find the best way to present, on stage, what they discover. At every step along the way, the actors reassess whether the material they are producing is true to life and whether it clearly communicates what they believe happens in the situations they are investigating. They complete their script, and when each actor performs, it is with the passion and authority of one who says, "This is how I see it; this is what I've created to help you understand what I see."

HOW THE BOOK IS ORGANIZED

Strategies for Playbuilding is divided into five parts. Part One, "Developing an Ensemble and Building Skills," begins with nine suggestions for specific steps to take during the first cast meeting. These steps will help establish an environment of respect, teamwork, and commitment among cast members. Part One also includes some general procedures for running the script development workshop sessions and offers examples of exercises designed to develop the actors' ensemble skills (confidence on stage, give-and-take) and imagination skills (thinking in visual terms). In each case, readers are shown the theory behind the exercise so that they can also invent their own exercises according to their group's needs. The section concludes with a description of an exercise called Investigating the Tools, which is one of the cornerstones of the script development process.

Part Two, "Identifying and Investigating the Topic," shows how to help the group choose a general topic and sort out those aspects of the topic that particularly fire their imaginations. It provides a series of exercises and worksheets designed to lead the group through the entire process of collaboratively unpacking stories drawn from their own experiences and research, clarifying their understanding, and transforming what they learn into evocative, theatrical terms: the raw material for their script.

Part Three, "Building Dialogue, Lyrics, and Choreography," clarifies some of the forms that dramatic and comic segments may take: scenes, monologues, songs, spoken choruses, and choreography. It provides suggestions for how to recombine the raw material into one or a combination of these forms and illustrates the process for each of the forms with an anecdotal example.

Part Four, "Weaving Individual Performance Pieces into a Show," is for those who want to create an entire production. It presents ideas on how to take stock of a variety of dramatic and comic segments and find a structure to make them all cohere. It also includes some guidelines on opening scenes, first act endings, and finales.

Part Five, "Rehearsing and Performing," has suggestions for some of the practical aspects of planning rehearsals, coaching actors, and staging a show.

Appendix A, "Tools," offers suggestions for starting a collection of materials in preparation for a script development project. Appendix B, "Auditions," presents ideas for recruiting actors and for conducting auditions that are not intimidating. Appendix C is a step-by-step process checklist. Appendix D is an annotated bibliography and resources section. Appendix E offers potential elements for a participant contract.

STRATEGIES FOR PLAYBUILDING

Helping Groups Translate Issues into Theatre

I would undertake to teach anyone all that I know about theatre rules and techniques in a few hours. The rest is practice . . .
Peter Brook

1 DEVELOPING AN ENSEMBLE AND BUILDING SKILLS

Everyone can do theatre—even actors!
Theatre can be done anywhere—even in theatres!
Augusto Boal

THE FIRST MEETING

The script development process described in this book is based on the principles of collaborative learning. In order for it to be effective, cast members must be willing to take individual responsibility for contributing to the project, but it is the director's job to set the tone for working well together. Here are nine suggestions for specific steps to take during the very first meeting to establish an environment of respect, teamwork, and commitment:

- sitting in a circle
- establishing a tone of respect
- establishing a sense of the group
- outlining the process
- considering measures of success
- setting up house rules, or promises to one another
- establishing systems for support and problem resolution
- respecting confidentiality and maintaining personal control of stories
- drawing up a contract.

Sitting in a Circle

| *What to do* Take time to arrange the seating in a circle rather than in rows facing front. If you are working in a comfortable room, you may even choose to have everyone, including the director(s), sit on the floor rather than in chairs.

| *Why* Simply put, a collaborative approach requires that everyone be able to see one another in order to freely exchange ideas. Chairs, especially those with built-in desktops, can tend to isolate, as if each person were in his own miniature castle. Sitting together on the floor is a subtle way to create a sense of connection among all the participants.

Establishing a Tone of Respect

| *What to do* Start off the first meeting by explicitly acknowledging the participants' initiative. They have come together to create a piece of theatre responding to a social issue that they feel is important. That means they are taking action to improve upon the way things are. They may seem at ease, but this project represents something new and, in a world of uncertainty, taking a risk on something new takes guts. Let them know that you respect them for their decision to be a part of this project and their willingness to do something that will make the school, the community, the world, a better place.

| *Why* There are lots of exercises designed to forge connections and build trust within a group; a few of them are described here. A little further along you'll be establishing systems for intragroup support and problem resolution. But a foundation of dignity and respect is the centerpiece of the whole works. Some of the participants may be primarily motivated by an interest in the topic; others may love to perform or have dreams of stardom; more than a few may simply see it as a fun or sociable activity. Whatever choices have brought them here, when you acknowledge the value of what they have to offer as intelligent, competent individuals and as artists, you set the stage for mutual respect.

Establishing a Sense of the Group

| *What to do* Ask the actors to take turns saying a few words about why they're here—what they hope to get from the project, why they want to do it, and what they feel they can contribute. Ask them to tell about one or two things that they're good at. Let them know it can be anything at all; it doesn't have to be related to theatre. If they don't already know one another, they can start off by saying their names.

As a part of the group, take your turn to tell what you hope to get from the project and what you feel you can contribute.

| *Why* Self-description not only provides an opportunity for individual validation but it also allows a sense of the group identity to emerge: its members, their strengths, and the commonality of their purpose. Their reasons for participating will vary, but they have all signed on to create a piece of theatre about an important issue. In both obvious and subtle ways, a sense of mission will surface as the actors identify some of the things that have drawn them to the project. That sense of purpose will help bond the group together from the beginning.

Outlining the Process

| *What to do* Take just a moment to give a brief outline of how the process is going to work. In your own words, explain the following points to the group.

First, they'll be doing some theatre exercises. Some of the exercises will get them used to working together as actors and some will give them practice turning ideas and discussions into theatre.

Second, if they haven't already chosen a topic, they'll decide what theme or issue they want to work on and they'll take a closer look at it. They'll take turns telling one another about things that have really happened, things they've personally seen or experienced that have to do with the topic. They may also decide to talk to other people and look at books, magazines, or videos to gather more stories about it.

Third, some theatre groups might act out the stories, but this group isn't going to. Instead of acting out what happened in one particular story, the group is going to look over all the different stories and figure out what they have in common. They'll turn that into theatre, songs, or choreography. Their performance will combine little bits and pieces from lots of stories to show the audience how this issue affects people and how people deal with it. Some may be serious, some may be funny, and some may be a little bit of both. Based on what they learn from the stories and what they already know, they'll be using theatre as a way to show *their* ideas about the way things are.

Finally, if you have one, give an idea of the time line for the project. Clarify how long each session will be and how much time is available for the script development workshops, rehearsals, and performances.

| ***Why*** The participants may have quite a range of assumptions and anxieties about the project they are about to begin. Helping them formulate a picture of what's ahead can put them at ease and will help them remain dedicated as they work through an unfamiliar process for the first time.

Some of the cast members may have entered into the project with a very specific agenda about teaching a moral or social lesson to their audience. Outlining the process early on can help those individuals understand that the intent of this work is different. It is less about telling what should happen or what is right and wrong than it is about showing what does happen. This approach to script development is founded upon a very basic premise: that as people try to improve a situation, disagreements about the best solution are often based on conflicting perceptions about the true nature of the problem. When young people put forward their understanding of what happens in social relationships, draw parallels that shed new light on familiar situations, and point out where they see preconceptions clouding the issue, they make a valuable contribution to their community. It is, in fact, a basic tenet of the creative problem-solving process that, as people become more conscious of what they are doing and how they are behaving, they become better able to change their behavior.[1] Young people can serve their communities well by helping their audiences reassess their assumptions and clear the way for creative action.

Considering Measures of Success

| ***What to do*** Ask the participants for their views on the purpose of the project. Who do they want to see their finished work? Another class? Younger students? Older students? The whole school? Their parents? The neighborhood? The city? Who in the city should see it? What would they

like to see happen because of what they do? How will they know if they've succeeded? Applause? Changed lives? How will they know if lives have been changed? Changed behaviors? What makes a show successful? Is it enough just to have a show that they feel proud of?

Why Some general attitudes about purpose were implied during the previous step, outlining the process. Still, whether conscious of it or not, the participants will naturally have their own ideas about the purpose of the project, how its success should be measured, and what their group's relationship to the audience will be. These unspoken assumptions and attitudes will have a subtle but profound effect on the shape of the work they do and their sense of accomplishment when it's over.

By talking about it, the group can make a deliberate choice. Together the participants can define goals and measures of success that are attainable. Also, reflecting as a group on the larger purpose of the project can give the cast a powerful sense of meaningful participation in the community. It helps them put their work into context. The work is not just about learning; it is about learning in order to communicate to others and contributing to the community dialogue.

From time to time through the course of the script development and rehearsal processes, you can help the actors renew their sense of purpose and dedication by taking time to review with them what they have accomplished so far and what lies ahead.

Setting Up House Rules, or Promises to One Another

What to do Propose to the group that rules can help people get along better because everyone knows exactly what's expected. You may choose to suggest to the group that everyone think of these not as rules, but as promises to one another. Ask for their opinions: "What promises should we make to one another?" Along with developing a list of promises, have the cast members work out a plan for consequences. What do they feel is a reasonable response if someone breaks a promise?

There are some good standard promises, such as "No put-downs." If no one else comes up with it, suggest this one and describe why it's important. If one person criticizes or laughs at another person's ideas, everyone will start to hold his ideas back, figuring somebody will make fun of them, too. But if everyone makes a promise to one another at the beginning that there will be no put-downs, there will be many more ideas to work with and everyone will have a lot more fun.

The group will probably come up with plenty of ideas for promises. Some may be redundant and can be fused with others. Generally speaking, a small number of clear basic promises is easier to handle than a whole constitution with multiple amendments. It may be helpful to write them up and post them in the room for easy reference.

Why It's self-evident that house rules about expectations are generally more effective when they are set up by the group itself rather than imposed from above. The semantic shift from "rules" to "promises to one another" can make a big difference. Rules can seem impersonal and tend to get bent and broken. Setting up promises to one another connects each rule directly to its effect on the other people in the group. Framing it this way can build upon everyone's integrity and sense of loyalty to one another.

Establishing Systems for Support and Problem Resolution

What to do In addition to defining basic, practical promises together, take a moment to lay some groundwork for intragroup support and problem resolution. You may find it effective to speak about this in terms of showing respect: respect for themselves, for one another, for the work, and for the space. Here are some suggestions you can pick from and put into your own words:

Respect Yourselves

- Each one of you has talent; each one of you has ideas to contribute that are valuable and important. Don't put yourself down, because you are what will make this project a success.
- In this room, with this group, show your best side. Help us respect you.
- Let us know if something's bothering you—if a friend is moving away or if you're worried about something that's just happened or is about to happen. Don't wait around feeling miserable until someone notices. Let us know that you've got something on your mind.
- We'll make time at the beginning of each session to check in with one another, to talk about how we're doing. If you don't feel comfortable telling everyone—if at any time there's something that's troubling you that you want to talk about privately—find me or one of the other teachers/staff members. We are here. If we can't stop what we're doing right then, we will stop long enough to set a time to talk with you later.

Respect One Another

- Take a minute to look around the room. You may already know everyone here; maybe there are some people you don't know. In a few weeks or months, these people will be your good friends. Treat them well now.
- Respect other people's space and their stuff. We've set up some promises to one another. They're good, but I think everyone knows deep down what's fair and what's not fair. If in doubt, be guided by that. Use your head.
- If you have a problem with someone, work it out. It doesn't help to go behind his back and complain about him to other people. Go to him first; lay it out for him to see what he's doing. You can say, "When you do ______, it makes me feel like ______, because ______. I'll give you an example: Let's say that Juliet and Romeo over here keep yakking during the workshop when I'm trying to explain something. Instead of just getting mad or complaining to my friends, I find some time to go

up to them and say, "WHEN YOU TWO keep talking after I've asked you to stop, IT MAKES ME FEEL LIKE you don't respect me, BECAUSE you're not listening to what I'm saying." Now they've been called on what they're doing, and it's up to them to change it.

Respect the Work

- We have a limited amount of time, so when your body is here, make sure your mind and your spirit are here, too. If you want to talk and catch up on what's happening with one another, please do it before we begin or after the session is over. Make a decision that, when we start, your attention is here with us.
- Also, we'll be working with a lot of stuff: props and fabrics and materials. We call them tools because we will use them to help make the play, just like you'd use tools to make a house. They can be fun to work with, but they're not playthings or weapons. Always remember to treat them carefully and safely.

Respect the Space

- At the end of every session, we need to leave the room in good shape. If you see a mess, even if it's not yours, take care of it. If it will help, we can set up a rotating crew so that everyone will take turns making sure the place is clean and orderly when we leave.

| *Why* You continue to set the tone for working well together by putting high expectations for behavior in terms of caring and support. Laying this groundwork gives participants some practical information about ways to obtain support and positive ways to respond to problems before troubles arise.

Respecting Confidentiality and Maintaining Personal Control of Stories

Two other critical points to stress are the importance of confidentiality and the veto option.

| *What to do* In your own words, communicate the following:

> I want to talk for a minute about confidentiality. That means that the stories stay in here. Outside of the group you are free to talk about what we're doing, the exercises, and how we're making the play. But people in the group will be telling stories about things that have happened to them or things they've seen. Some of the stories will be personal. As I said before, we're not going to act out these stories, but we're going to learn from them. We're going to use them to figure out how people deal with different situations. I ask that you never repeat other people's stories outside this room unless they *clearly* give their permission to you. It's called confidentiality because we're confiding in one another, and that means

each of us trusts that what we say is not going to get around as gossip. Can everyone agree to that?

That brings me to the other thing I want to talk about. It's called veto power. Toward the end of the scripting workshops, if something about a story you told made it into the script, and you feel it's too personal, you have veto power. You can say, "I'd rather that part not be in there," and it will come out. All I ask is that you not censor it at the beginning. Sometimes you might feel awkward about sharing a story because you think it's too weird or too embarrassing. You might be surprised to find that a lot of other people have had similar experiences or feel exactly the same way you do. Test it out. Share it with us. Then, later, if you think about it and you feel that something you said needs to be taken out of the script, we will take it out. No arguments.

| ***Why*** It is very likely that the participants will be dealing with issues that reach deeply into their personal lives. They will be using this script development process to gain some perspective on their life experiences and those of their peers. Obviously, individuals will be more willing to share information about themselves if they feel assured that it won't be broadcast to the general community and if they know that they ultimately retain the power to retract it from the final script. This means, if an actor chooses to pull something from the script, no matter how artistically dazzling it might be, the director must honor that request without trying to overrule, negotiate, or plead. No arguments.

Drawing Up a Contract

Finally, you may choose to write up a contract that clearly delineates the expectations and consequences the group has discussed, along with a schedule or general timetable for the project. Cast members should know that participation requires a commitment of attending regularly, avoiding tardiness, and remaining drug- and alcohol-free. While grades may go up as a result of the mental exercises and positive experience, grades that go down could indicate that extra time spent in theatre is interfering with schoolwork, and cast members and directors should try to strike a balance between the two. An agreement of understanding between the director and each cast member, cosigned by a parent or guardian, establishes this commitment.

| ***Why*** A contract serves several purposes. In addition to making the specific expectations absolutely clear, it allows the families of cast members to learn something about the project and the amount of time it will involve. It gives them the opportunity literally and figuratively to sign on to the project with their support. A written contract also reinforces a sense of exclusivity about the project. It sends a signal to cast members and their families that this project is a serious endeavor. A model of some elements to include in a written contract can be found in Appendix E.

How Much Time Does It Take?

There is no standard amount of time required to complete this script development and rehearsal process. To a large degree it depends upon the scope of the project, which can range from the development of a short song or scene to that of a full-length musical production. The more ambitious the project, the more time it will take. To create a ninety-minute musical show with a multiage group of twenty to twenty-five young people and an artistic staff (music, choreography, etc.), I try to schedule fifty to sixty hours of script development workshop sessions and forty to fifty hours of rehearsal time. On the other hand, I once worked with a multiage cast of ten kids already familiar with the process and was able to help them create a powerful thirty-second public service announcement on AIDS/HIV awareness in about four hours (not counting time editing the video—they produced too much material!). If you are concerned about not being able to complete a project in the limited amount of time available, start working on a small scale and plan to expand. The group can begin by creating individual, focused elements: a song, a scene, or a piece of choreography. Then, depending upon the pace of their work, they can create more. In general, the script development sessions will take a little more time than the rehearsals, since by the time the actors reach the rehearsal stage they are already familiar with the material they've created.

THE SCRIPT DEVELOPMENT WORKSHOP SESSIONS

When working with a group of individuals who are new to one another, I have found it very effective for them to engage in some general team building right from the start. Some directors may be able to arrange for the group to participate in an increasingly popular activity called a challenge course or ropes course. These programs are full- or half-day sessions led by trained facilitators who take groups through a series of (usually outdoor) physical problem-solving exercises all designed to inspire a team effort and build understanding of how to work collaboratively. Alternatively, you may choose to lead the group yourself. There are several outstanding books on the market with information on how to facilitate team-building activities. Taking a day or so for this work at the beginning of a project, whether inside or outside the classroom, can go a long way toward building a sense of family among members of the group.

An annotated list of some books on the subject and contact information for availability and locations of challenge/ropes courses throughout the world can be found in the resources section at the back of the book (Appendix D).

Check-In Time

Take a few minutes at the beginning of each session for a brief check-in to keep lines of communication open. It doesn't take long to go around the circle and ask how everybody is doing and how everyone is feeling about the work.

Warm-Ups

After checking in, have everyone stand up, still in a circle, for a brief physical and vocal warm-up. A warm-up not only serves to limber the body and voice, it helps the participants become present. A little physical exertion provides a palpable break between whatever they have just come from and the work they are about to start. It doesn't need to be complicated; a very simple series of stretches will do nicely. They might begin by dropping heads forward and then rolling them around to the side, back, other side, and to the front again. They can repeat and then roll their heads in the other direction. They can then extend their arms straight out to the sides, being careful to allow enough room so that no one hits a neighbor. They can now draw little circles in the air with their fists, first going forward, then backward. The circles they draw in the air can get larger. Elbows and shoulders can draw a circle in the air, first forward, then backward. Extending one leg at a time in front of themselves and rotating at the ankle, they can draw a small circle with their toes clockwise, then counterclockwise. They can draw circles large and small in both directions with the knee and then the entire leg. They can splay their fingers, then make a fist, splay them again and then shake them out. They can stretch their faces and jaws round and round and side to side. With feet on the ground and legs a bit apart, they can all drop forward at the waist and hang with arms limp. They can take a few breaths and then, starting at the base of the spine, slowly stand upright, stacking one vertebra on top of another, finishing with the neck, until they are all looking forward.

A vocal warm-up can be very simple, too. The group can find a high note together—*aaaaahhhhhh*—and then exhale in unison, dropping together through the scale to a low note. Then everyone can go from low notes to high notes together. A warm-up leader with an improvisational bent can play around with a scat singing style: *woh-bah-day-bah-doo-bah-dee-bah-dah-bah-dah*, spontaneously making up words and tunes that the group then repeats in unison (or individually when pointed to), line by line.

You can develop a basic physical/vocal warm-up routine such as this one, with room for variations. All of the actors can learn it and they can each take turns leading the warm-up from one session to the next. There may well be individuals in your group who are dancers, singers, actors, or athletes and have some previous experience in warming up. By all means let them introduce their own material.

Tumbling

Simple acrobatic and tumbling exercises can have a remarkably beneficial effect on actors. Nicola Savarse has described how the act of completing these exercises helps performers develop their stage presence:

> The acrobatic exercise gives the performer the opportunity to test his power. At first, the exercise is used to help him overcome fear and resistance, to help him overcome his limits; later, it becomes a way of controlling apparently uncontrollable energies, of finding, for example, the counter impulses necessary to fall without hurting oneself or of gliding through the air in defiance of the law of gravity. Above and beyond the exercise, these victories reassure the performer: "Even if I don't do it, I am *able* to do it." And on stage, because of this knowledge, the body becomes a *decided* body.[2]

Successfully learning to execute even simple things, like somersaults, cartwheels, and headstands, can give young actors a confidence that reaches into every other part of their theatre work. Dive rolls, running dive rolls (or tiger leaps), and handsprings take more time to master, and the payoff is proportionally as great. There are books on the subject of teaching these skills, but opinions about what constitutes a safe and correct technique have changed dramatically in recent years. If you would like to try introducing these skills but you don't feel confident teaching them yourself, you may be able to find an experienced tumbling or gymnastics teacher willing to volunteer a little instruction time with your cast.

Singing

If at all possible, spend just a little time at the beginning of each session singing together as a group. There is a rich connection forged when people sing together and it is certainly worth the effort it takes to build a singing component into your allotted time. For those who become absolutely unglued at the thought of singing in public, I recommend Nick Page's inspiring book *Sing and Shine On: The Teacher's Guide to Multicultural Song Leading*. It is, in fact, a fine resource for anyone seeking to integrate singing into their work with students. Looking for songs to sing? Get a copy of *Rise Up Singing: The Group Singing Songbook*. This exciting compendium was put together by Peter Blood and Annie Patterson and published by Sing Out. It features the words, chords, and sources for twelve hundred songs in thirty-five categories, all indexed by title, artist, subject, cultures (languages, nationalities, etc.), and more. The book is specifically designed for nonprofessionals who want to sing together, and just flipping through its pages is enough to get a person going. Still anxious? If all else fails, there may actually be some singers in the cast. There's no reason that they shouldn't teach some of the songs they know and lead the others.

Journals

There will be a lot of ideas, discussions, participatory research, and gathering of material during the weeks ahead. For that reason, you should encourage the actors to keep workshop journals. Participants can fill the journals with ideas and thoughts that occur within the workshops or at random times of the day or evening when they are reflecting on the project. They can later use the journals for rehearsal notebooks. Ideas slip in and out of our heads, and establishing a specific place to note them down can really help the cast members make sense of their work. Make it clear that their journals won't be checked for spelling or grammar. The purpose is to get the ideas down, not to create a formal presentation.

The actors can also use the pages for quick writes. At various points during the workshops, such as directly following an activity or a guest presentation and before opening a discussion, you can have the actors turn to their journals to write down a few quick individual responses. These quick writes can help ensure that everyone, not just the more outgoing and verbal members of the cast, has something to contribute to the subsequent discussion.

Concentration

Many directors work with actors on focus. When attention or energy lags, the familiar mantra is heard: "Focus, everyone, let's keep focused!" But it can be limiting. It is, after all, a negative objective. The actor intent on focusing is trying to shut out everything, to put on blinders and direct his attention to one place only. The trouble is that there is so much competition for attention, both inside his brain and outside in the room, that the blinders just keep falling off.

An alternative approach is to give them a positive objective. It has been described in many different theatrical traditions: A *fictive* body. Being at rest, not relaxed. A *decided* body. Present, not absent. The French term is *dans le jeu*, which translates to *in the game*. That's an easy one to understand—being in the game versus not in the game. When you're in it, you're playing. You're thinking about your teammates and about the task. Instead of shutting everything out, you're taking everything in. You are alert and aware of your surroundings. It is an important distinction. Instead of being told to narrow his focus, the actor is encouraged to tune in to everything around him. Then he'll be ready to respond to whatever happens.

By giving the actors a positive objective, you can encourage that sensation among the actors when they're working. Whenever the actors gather to try out an exercise, get them accustomed to standing on the balls of their feet, as if they'd be able to move in any direction on a split second's notice. Make it your group code that dans le jeu, or in the game, or whatever phrase you prefer, signifies a reminder for the actors to shift into that state.

Physical Confidence Exercises

Most of the exercises described here are intended to encourage the development of a strong ensemble of actors by developing their sense of confidence. There is a tendency among young or inexperienced actors to wander and mumble on stage. These performers exhibit a lack of physical confidence in themselves and only a vague connection to their fellow actors. By contrast, in any group of kids playing an active team sport, there will be plenty of players who assertively charge at the ball, fairly well aware of their kinesthetic relationships to the other kids on the team. The young athletes have had drills in which they've practiced their skills and developed confidence in their own abilities and in the abilities of their teammates. What the young actors need are practice drills in which they, too, can develop confidence in themselves and in their teammates when they are on stage. They need opportunities to test out their personal capacity to commit themselves both physically and imaginatively and to enjoy some success. That confidence in themselves and in one another will ultimately give them presence and connection in performance. It will also help them to create bolder and more dynamic work as they develop their script, lyrics, or choreography.

What follows are six exercises that promote confidence by way of physical commitment.[3] The first two exercises involve only a slight physical commitment. They are good for getting the actors started. These exercises prevent the actors from making judgments and holding back by introducing simple physical tasks that also require some mental dexterity. Participants become engaged in the task and lose track of the fact that they're committing themselves. The next two exercises require the actors to initiate some more involved physical action and to react and respond to the other actors. Finally, there are two exercises that involve actors working one-on-one with other actors. These exercises promote the actors' confidence about working with partners. At the end of each exercise is a suggestion for ways in which the reader can invent more exercises along the same lines as the ones described.

Those looking for a greater selection of physical theatre exercises will find a helpful source in section three of the book *Games for Actors and Non-Actors* by Augusto Boal and the books by Karl Rohnke listed in Appendix D.

Following are examples of exercises involving slight physical commitment.

Group Juggle

This exercise requires three or more beanbags, although socks filled with a cup of dried peas or beans and then knotted will do just fine.

| *What to do* Standing in a circle, one actor in the group tosses a beanbag—nice and easy and underhand—to the person who is standing just to the *right* of whomever is directly across from him. In order to get the receiver's attention, he calls her name and makes sure she hears him before he tosses her the beanbag. If he doesn't know her name, he first needs to ask her what it is. After she catches it, she tosses the beanbag to the person standing across the circle who is just to the right of the person who threw it to her. She likewise calls his name and makes sure he's heard her and knows it's coming. He catches it and tosses it to the right of the person who threw it to him, and so forth. Once the beanbag has gone around the circle, add another beanbag, and then another. Each actor will have beanbags coming from every direction, always preceded by a tosser calling the receiver's name. Once the group becomes adept, you can increase the challenge by adding more bags or selectively alternating directions. For example, you could say the yellow beanbag must be tossed to the right of the person who tossed it, but the red beanbag should be tossed to the left, and so forth. If someone drops a beanbag, no harm done, he just picks it up and tosses it back into the mix.

There is no naturally obvious ending to this exercise. It will often just fizzle out when the majority of the beanbags accidentally land on the ground. To make it end on a more triumphant note, you can call out: "On the count of three, toss the beanbags into the center of the circle and reach up and take one another's hands. One . . . two . . . three!"

| ***Why*** The task of tossing and catching a beanbag across a circle is fairly easy. So is the one (initial) rule of throwing it to the right of the person who threw it to you. Starting with one beanbag gives the participants a chance to get the hang of it slowly. But before long, the relentlessness of the arriving beanbags makes it impossible for a mind to wander. The air is full of flying objects. Everyone's peripheral vision is wide open. Where did that one come from? Where is this one going? When no one is dropping the beanbags, especially if they're brightly colored, the exercise can be pretty spectacular and exhilarating. In addition, a Group Juggle is a good way to learn names.

To design exercises along the lines of a Group Juggle, come up with two or more repeatable physical or verbal tasks that are easy to perform by themselves but which are different enough as to make it challenging to perform them together. Start with one, and then gradually introduce the other(s).

Human Knot

| ***What to do*** This exercise works best with six to ten people. If the group is larger than that, divide it into two or more smaller groups. Standing in a very tight circle, shoulder to shoulder, each person takes the hands of two others who are *not* standing next to him. The actors are now in a circle of people holding hands and twisted into a human knot. The task is to work out how to untwist the knot without letting go of hands, by ducking under and stepping over arms. To increase the challenge, they can do this exercise without using their voices to communicate.

| ***Why*** Subtle dynamics of leadership and cooperation come into play whenever a group tries to work out the solution to a problem. With a Human Knot, those social dynamics become easy to see. Solving the problem requires everyone's participation. Competing or pushy leaders make

the task more difficult. The more times the participants try this exercise, the better they become at collaboratively negotiating the solution to a problem. If, after each time they do it, the participants take a moment to reflect on how the exercise went, they will improve their ability to gauge how they are working as a group. That awareness will help them improve their collaborative skills the next time around.

To design exercises along the lines of a Human Knot, come up with a physical task that will require the entire group to work together to achieve. Give them a certain period of time to solve the problem. Be sure to take time afterward for the group to reflect on how the exercise went.

Following are examples of exercises involving more physical commitment.

Camera Above

| ***What to do*** Tell the actors to imagine that there is a camera on the ceiling looking straight down at them. Explain that you will call out various shapes and they must quickly move so everybody forms that shape for the camera above. Then call out shapes such as the capital letter *M* or the lowercase letter *b*; a square or a circle; the number 5 or the number 63; and so on. As soon as they've successfully assumed one shape, call out another shape. You can increase the challenge by introducing a time limit and loudly counting down from ten or five to zero as soon as you announce the shape.

| ***Why*** The actors are provided with the goal of the task; to create a shape as seen from above. But unlike the Human Knot, a central piece of information about the task—the specific shape to assume—is withheld until the last minute. The exercise allows them time to learn the rules and to feel confident in knowing what they are supposed to do but denies them the opportunity to plan out a solution together. They become physically engaged in quickly solving a problem as a group with no time for debate or discussion.

To design exercises along the lines of Camera Above, come up with a physical task that will require the entire group to work together to achieve. As you give the instructions, withhold some critical piece of information about the task so that the group becomes confident about knowing what it is supposed to do but cannot carry it out until you supply that final piece of information. The piece of information may be a limitation (accomplish the task without using hands, for example), or it may involve some specificity (for example, they know they will create something, but not specifically what it will be).

Sound and Movement

| ***What to do*** The actors stand in a circle. A volunteer steps into the center and initiates a single repeatable body movement and vocalized sound. It can be anything at all—a realistic gesture and a word or something completely abstract and wild. After she's repeated it several times, someone else from the circle steps in to accurately reproduce it with his body and voice.

The two are now repeating the sound and movement in tandem. The first actor waits until the second is doing it exactly right. When she is satisfied that he's got it down, she stops and rejoins the circle. He continues for a moment with hers. Then, without pause, he shifts to his own movement and sound. Someone else steps forward to reproduce it alongside him and the exercise continues. Some participants may be timid and produce only a little gesture and a hushed or squeaky vocal sound. During a second round, you can gently encourage them to be bolder in their movement and fuller in their voice.

| *Why* In the previous exercises, the actors received opportunities to test out physically committing themselves as part of a group. In Sound and Movement, the actors test out physically committing themselves individually. That can be intimidating, but the way the exercise is designed, they are not alone for long and for the most part, their focus is not on themselves. With the exception of the first volunteer, each person's time in the center of the circle is divided between duplicating another actor's work—taking from a partner—and offering work—giving to a partner. The moment between is fixed and brief, and in that moment of dropping the adopted sound and movement and initiating a new one, the actors get to test out their capacity to overcome hesitancy. They get a chance to be bold. The simplicity of having to produce only a single, repeatable sound and movement makes it easier to achieve than a more complicated presentation would be.

This exercise promotes two different skills: the capacity to physically commit and sensitivity to what another actor is doing. To design exercises along the lines of the former, you might rely on tumbling exercises as described earlier. As the actors feel more comfortable committing themselves, come up with tasks that require them to be bigger than life, such as crossing a room taking up as much space as possible, individually or in pairs. To design exercises along the lines of the latter, come up with tasks that require the actors to observe and reproduce something (the way a particular person or animal walks, etc.) and then demonstrate and teach it to the other actors.

Following are examples of exercises involving partner work.

Mirrors

| *What to do* Working in pairs, the actors face each other. One begins a movement and the partner operates as a reflection, physically mirroring everything the first actor does. The first actor never tries to trick the mirror into making a wrong move but aims to enable the mirror to reflect each action exactly. After a while, the director calls out for the two to switch roles and, without a break, the second actor takes over initiating action and the first actor begins to mirror.

| *Why* Mirror exercises continue the development of sensitivity and awareness to others, which was begun in the Sound and Movement exercise, but with more subtlety. More importantly, mirror exercises can help inexperienced actors overcome qualms about personal distance. The actors need to become comfortable with relating to one another physically. Unwritten social rules about proximity need to be addressed by actors who may ultimately be picking each other up and helping one another move through space. These unwritten rules about personal distance are easy to demonstrate. If two volunteers are asked to stand eye-to-eye, anxiety about proximity becomes dramatically clear, for both the participants and the observers. For some, that kind of closeness carries a connotation of intimacy or threat. You can use the Mirrors exercise as an opportunity to talk with the actors about the need to put aside those connotations while working on the project. Make it clear that everyone knows there are inappropriate places to touch other people and that everyone must be respectful of those areas but, generally speaking, they can be next to each other and even be in physical contact, knowing that later on it's not going to mean anything—because they are actors and they were acting.

To design exercises along the lines of Mirrors, come up with other ways in which actors must pay close attention to what one another is doing. A vocal variation on Mirrors is called Simultaneous Translation. Working in pairs face-to-face, one actor talks about anything at all and the other tries, like a United Nations translator, to repeat what the first actor is saying as she is saying it. A group variation of Mirrors involves having the actors sit in a circle. One actor initiates a rhythm by clapping hands. All the others follow suit, clapping with the same rhythm at the same time. At any point, the one who initiated the rhythm changes it and the others attempt to follow the switch without missing a beat. This exercise becomes more challenging if the identity of the one initiating the clapping rhythm is unknown, having been secretly selected by you.

Counterweights

For safety's sake, first ask two volunteers to demonstrate this exercise for the rest of the group. They follow the instructions while everyone watches to see how it is done. When the demonstration is over, everyone finds a partner and tries out the exercise in pairs.

| *What to do* Facing each other with toes touching toes, the actors each extend a hand as if to shake hands, but they instead take hold of the other's wrist—this offers more support than taking hold of hands in handshake fashion. Each actor's free hand hangs at her side. Keeping legs straight, they both slowly lean back, extending the arm that is holding the other person's wrist. They are now creating a V, supporting each other's weight. If they wish, they can now bend their knees into a squat, still leaning back and extending their free hands behind them for extra balance. When they are ready, they straighten their knees and slowly rise, pulling their partners up straight again and then letting go of their partner's wrist. As they become comfortable with this exercise, the two partners can release their grip for just a second once they pull each other up to a vertical position and then gracefully switch hands and lean back again. They pull each other up, switch, and lean back again.

| Why Like many trust exercises, Counterweights requires one actor to support another. What makes this one interesting is that the partners rely on each other equally. There is no truster and trustee. In order to succeed, both partners use their weight to counterbalance the other. It is physically impossible to lean so far back without a partner to support you. If either were to let go, they both would fall, but neither lets go. The physics of the exercise allow for partners of very different heights and weights to work together; the V just becomes tilted on its axis so that the smaller, lighter-weight person leans farther back. This exercise gives actors a chance to enjoy the fun of a small victory over gravity, which is clearly achieved only via partnership with another actor. It forges a connection of trust. As a more advanced variation, the actors can walk around the room, extend hands as if to shake them in greeting, grip wrists, and lean back. They then pull up to vertical again and let go. They continue to walk around the room, find another person, extend hands to that one, and repeat.

To design exercises along the lines of Counterweights, come up with ways for partners or groups of three or more to rely on one another for balance. Some familiar variations include standing back-to-back, inching down to a sitting position, then returning to a standing position or standing side by side holding wrists and leaning away from one another.

Troubleshooting

If some cast members are consistently unwilling to become involved, take them aside for a talk. Many young people have had to put up pretty tough veneers just to survive. In a private conversation you can acknowledge that you understand the importance of keeping up one's guard in some situations, but go on to suggest that this situation is different—those rules don't apply here. What happens in this group is different from what happens on the street or in the hallways. Talk about what the actor wants from this project and what the rest of the group wants. If the two are truly irreconcilable, it will be obvious. If, however, there is some meeting point, even a small one, you can ask him to give it a chance for a while, to join in and see how it goes. Make it clear that you believe that he can do this work.

Incorporating Physical Virtuosity

| What to do Pass out copies of the Inventory of Skills worksheet (see p. 20) and discuss the meaning of the word *inventory*. Participants who have worked in a store will be familiar with it. They'll know that the reason for taking an inventory is to get an accurate list of all the things a store has. Explain that each person in the group has skills, things each is good at, and the worksheets will help them make an accurate list of all the skills the group has. When they start to make theatre, they won't just be using words, they'll be using whatever they can think of to help them put their ideas on stage. If they know about all the skills available within the group, they can make use of those skills to create a performance that is exciting and interesting.

Ask everyone to take a few minutes to complete a worksheet and then go through the list together skill by skill. Invite cast members to indicate which of the boxes they've marked and to elaborate where appropriate—type of musical instruments played, other talents, and so on. The worksheets can be collected and made available for later reference as needed.

Throughout the course of the script development workshop sessions, set aside times for the participants to demonstrate their skills for one another, in a sort of mini talent show. If some individuals find they want to learn a skill that has piqued their interest, they can track down a how-to book on the subject or seek out local experts or fellow cast members to teach a particular skill to them or the entire group.

| *Why* Invariably, participants will possess a high degree of physical ability in one thing or another outside the realm of what are considered theatre skills. The worksheets will help them broaden their own conceptions of the useful talents they possess and periodic demonstrations will remind them of the pool of talents they can draw upon. There is tremendous audience appeal in displays of skill on stage. By integrating impressive feats of physical virtuosity into their work, the actors can capitalize on that appeal while at the same time presenting complex ideas in visually and aurally exciting ways.

Consider, for example, if several cast members were athletes skilled at throwing or catching a ball. They may not associate that particular ability with their theatre work but they could use those skills to create a breathtaking bit of choreography, deftly passing or tossing a variety of objects to one another through the air. Many athletic skills are wonderfully applicable to staging. I worked on a high school production of *The Wizard of Oz* in which we determined through a quick survey that a dozen cast members were talented roller skaters. This was before the era of roller blades. On opening night, those twelve actors donned their simian paper mache half masks, strapped on their foam rubber wings, and laced up their skates. The audience was dazzeled and thrilled by a troupe of flying monkeys that flew off ramps and zoomed around the stage in complex patterns bedeviling Dorothy and her companions. In that production, it turned out that the actor playing the Wicked Witch of the West was a long time aficionado of the trampoline. We set up a small trampoline anchored just offstage. For her first entrance, she used it as a springboard to catapult herself over a three-foot-high set piece at the edge of the stage, arriving in Munchinkinland from above.

Some skills and talents among the cast members will be less flashy, but no less useful. For example, in the Family and Cultural Traditions section on the Inventory of Skills worksheet, participants are asked to identify skills they have learned from their families. I once worked with a cast that wanted to create a scene dealing with the isolating and intimidating experience of arriving into a new and unfamiliar culture. Two of the actors were originally from South Korea and they shared with the rest of us a sweet and simple Korean song they both knew from childhood. We designed a medley in which the singer of that song had to compete vocally with a far more boisterous American children's song being sung by a chorus of full-throated and enthusiastic American kids. It proved to be a very eloquent way to present the gut feelings of that experience on stage. Here, again, the idea was prompted by an initial assessment of the actors' skills and talents.

Cast members building a script together will find helpful building blocks in their fellow actors' abilities to play an instrument, to sing, hum, whistle or even make vocal sound effects. A student musician who may or may not be able to perform Mozart can support the tension of a scene with a few notes on her bass or break that tension with a few notes on his piccolo. More experienced musicians or vocalists will be able to offer more complex musical contributions. Actors skilled at making vocal sound effects might be drafted to create a variation on what direct Joseph Chaikin called sound summaries, spontaneously creating the ambient sounds where a scene takes place. With a little practice, a small group of actors can use their voices to evoke the aural environment of, say, a sporting event: the squeak of sneakers and thump of the ball on the basketball court, the sounds of the players, the crowds in the bleachers, the whistle of the referee. According to the needs of the script, they can be called upon to create the ambient sounds of other places: a city sidewalk at rush hour, a small town road at dusk, a religious service or school detention room.

Remarkable displays of physical virtuosity are often used solely to wow spectators with the skill of the performer. We've all seen jugglers and acrobats and musicians who leave us shaking our heads in wonder at their sheer talent. That is not the aim of this work. In this arena, the performers' talents are used to highlight and reveal meaning. As the cast members create their script and staging, incorporating dynamic elements allows them to add texture and depth and excitement to what they want to communicate to their audience.

Inventory of Skills

Name: ____________________

Mark the first box for *I can do it.*
Mark the second box for *I am pretty good at it.*
Mark the third box for *I am very good at it.*

Voice

Whistling or Humming

☐ ☐ ☐ Can you whistle tunes?
☐ ☐ ☐ hum tunes?
☐ ☐ ☐ make loud whistles (with or without fingers)?

Imitations

☐ ☐ ☐ Can you imitate the way other people talk (voices of famous people or people you know)?

Sound Effects

☐ ☐ ☐ Can you make sound effects with your voice?

Speaking

☐ ☐ ☐ Are you good at reading out loud?
☐ ☐ ☐ Are you good at telling jokes?
☐ ☐ ☐ Are you good at reciting poems?
☐ ☐ ☐ Are you good at telling stories?
☐ ☐ ☐ Are you good at reciting poems?
☐ ☐ ☐ Are you good at memorizing words to songs, jokes, poems, or a part in a play?

Do you know more than one language? Which language(s)?

☐ ☐ ☐ ____________________

☐ ☐ ☐ ____________________

Physical Coordination

Can you do a

☐ ☐ ☐ somersault?
☐ ☐ ☐ handstand?
☐ ☐ ☐ cartwheel?
☐ ☐ ☐ backward handstand?
☐ ☐ ☐ headstand?
☐ ☐ ☐ dive roll?

Can you perform any other tumbling or acrobatic feat(s)? Please list them.

☐ ☐ ☐ ____________________

☐ ☐ ☐ ____________________

Are you good on wheels?

☐ ☐ ☐ skateboard
☐ ☐ ☐ roller skates
☐ ☐ ☐ inline skates
☐ ☐ ☐ bicycle
☐ ☐ ☐ scooter
☐ ☐ ☐ unicycle

Do you dance? What kind of dancing do you prefer?

☐ ☐ ☐ ____________________

☐ ☐ ☐ ____________________

Are there any other special physical skills you can do?

☐ ☐ ☐ rope skipping/jumping

☐ ☐ ☐ juggling

☐ ☐ ☐ stilt walking

☐ ☐ ☐ baton twirling

☐ ☐ ☐ catching (a ball or object)

☐ ☐ ☐ throwing (a ball or object)

☐ ☐ ☐ other ____________________

Imitations

☐ ☐ ☐ Can you imitate the way other people walk (famous people or people you know)?

Music

Do you sing? What kind of songs are you good at singing?

☐ ☐ ☐ ____________________

☐ ☐ ☐ ____________________

Do you play any musical instruments? What kind?

☐ ☐ ☐ ____________________

☐ ☐ ☐ ____________________

☐ ☐ ☐ Are you good at making rhythm with your hands (clapping or drumming on things)?

Art/Design

Do you

☐ ☐ ☐ draw?

☐ ☐ ☐ make things with clay?

☐ ☐ ☐ paint?

☐ ☐ ☐ make things from wood or metal?

☐ ☐ ☐ Are you good at lettering (making signs)?

Is there some other kind of art or design you do? Please explain.

☐ ☐ ☐ ____________________

Family and Cultural Traditions

Are there things you can do that you have learned from your family? Please explain.

☐ ☐ ☐ ____________________

☐ ☐ ☐ ____________________

Other Skills or Talents

Are there other things you are good at that you would like to mention? (It can be anything at all!)

☐ ☐ ☐ ____________________

☐ ☐ ☐ ____________________

Imagination Exercises

Above and beyond confidence-building exercises, there are important exercises designed to foster use of the imagination. Specifically, these exercises help the actors become accustomed to the idea of thinking in visual terms.

Astonishing Things

| *What to do* Tell the actors you want them to start exercising their imaginations by thinking about things they have seen in their lives that were astonishing. Ask them to define what they think the word *astonishing* means, and then as a group make up a list of astonishing things the actors have witnessed. Post the list in the room and encourage them to keep adding to it as more ideas occur to them over time.

| *Why* The first step toward deliberately designing evocative, compelling material for the stage is to conceptualize what is evocative and compelling. This exercise will quickly begin to help the actors get the idea. The power of these images can be pretty universal. I once worked with a group of elementary school students who, at ages seven and eight, identified more than a half-dozen astonishing things that would without question capture the imagination of mature adults:

seeing someone you love being hurt
falling through space
seeing someone very young do a really good job
seeing something moving that's not really alive
being stuck upside down
doctors using needles and thread to fix people
breaking your leg on your birthday
a beautiful thing, like a canopy bed

As the actors consider the question "What is astonishing?" over the course of the workshops, they will gradually improve their ability to pick out what specifically it is about something that they believe makes it astonishing. Both consciously and unconsciously, they'll start to integrate visually and aurally striking elements into their creative work.

This Shows Who I Am

| *What to do* Ask each cast member to bring in a personal item that she feels shows something about who she is, and have her explain its significance to the rest of the group.

| *Why* In part, this exercise provides another opportunity for individual self-validation. But by using objects to help communicate meaning, the actors also develop their facility for linking intangible concepts to tangible things. This exercise leads directly into other kinds of imagination work with objects.

Make This into Something It's Not

| *What to do* Have the actors sit in a circle and quickly pass a bandanna from person to person. Ask each one to make the bandanna into something it's not. After a few rounds, a few found (commonplace) objects are introduced such as a funnel, a vegetable steamer, and so forth. The operative word here is *quickly*. There should not be any thoughtful pondering about what will be the most clever choice. Instruct them to make the bandanna or object into the first thing that pops into their heads when it is passed to them.

A bandanna or a found object can be surprisingly evocative of an incredible range of other things. Bandannas are vague enough in shape to be almost anything: a bird, a snake, a flower, dripping snot, a miniature baseball diamond, the rope used by a right and left hand engaged in a tug-of-war. In contrast, each of the found objects has qualities that make it unique. The cast members start to pick out the specific aspects of an object that distinguish it. Those unique qualities affect their decision to make it into one thing rather than another. The funnel becomes a trumpet, a Valkyrie's breastplate, a way to get lots of food in the mouth. The steamer is folded and unfolded to become a satellite dish, a 1940s radio microphone, a flying saucer, or a goalie's hockey mask.

| *Why* On a basic level, the exercise lets the actors simply enjoy the fun of discovering how much potential for creative invention there is in a single ordinary object. But more importantly, the development of this kind of perceptual awareness serves as a warm-up to the next stage of the process: choosing and manipulating objects to deliberately communicate meaning on stage.

Investigating the Tools

This exercise is one of the cornerstones of the script development process. After it is first introduced, it can be used in every subsequent session as a warm-up. Although I have often had actors generate images during the exercise that were subsequently used in shows, the primary purpose of the work is for them to cultivate a way of seeing. Within the confines of the exercise, it doesn't matter how relevant the meaning is. In the beginning, actors just fiddle around with images to discover what they can communicate. With practice, they find it easier and easier to deliberately create stage moments that evoke subtle and specific shades of meaning.

The Investigating the Tools exercise relies on the use of props and common found objects, pieces of fabric, and even small musical instruments. It will require gathering a collection of these things. I refer to the whole assortment of stuff as tools. In part, this is to encourage the actors to handle with care what might otherwise be considered a bunch of secondhand junk; as tools they deserve some respect. But the term also promotes the idea that these common objects can be used to communicate meaning. An object is just an object; a tool is used to build something.

While you can encourage the actors to find and bring in items they'd like to contribute to the collection, it is a good idea to start off by gathering a healthy assortment yourself ahead of time. With a little scouting around, you can pick up many things for zero to nominal cost. Others may require some spending. A trip to the local recycling center, junkyard, or thrift store can yield lots of possibilities. Objects considered too banged up or broken for their intended use are ideal for tools. Appendix A has a description of the kinds of tools I've found to be particularly useful.

Why Use Props?

The theatre term *prop* is, of course, shorthand for *stage property*. It usually refers to objects carried by the characters in a play. However, when it comes to developing original script material with a group of actors, another definition of the term takes on particular significance. Prop also means to support, as in *to prop up*.

How does an object give support? By providing something to lean on. When focused on a prop, the actor feels less vulnerable and is able to take bigger risks. In the theatre, generally speaking, the actor's body is his instrument of expression. But untrained actors, unfamiliar with one another and the director, may show some reluctance to commit themselves physically and emotionally.

Consider the following scenario: An actor is asked to demonstrate to the rest of the group her perceptions about a relationship or social situation. She gets up in front of the group and she is understandably nervous about potential failure and criticism. Her focus is on herself, on what she is doing. Our focus is on her. Not wanting to look foolish, she checks herself and takes only a small risk, demonstrating a little gesture or a phrase that captures the quality of the event. Alternatively, the same actor is asked to go to a large pile of fabric pieces, various found objects, and simple musical instruments and pick out one or two things to help her demonstrate a relationship or social situation. She can choose to manipulate them like a puppeteer, or she can use them in relation to her own body or between herself and another actor. Suddenly the focus—both ours and hers—switches to the objects. The props have provided a boundary around her presentation that allows her to more easily delineate between the idea she is demonstrating and herself personally. Additionally, the objects themselves have the capacity to extend her range of expressiveness and to help her articulate subtle meaning. She finds herself freed up, physically and emotionally. Moreover, her colleagues' feedback focuses on the relative effectiveness of her artistic choices rather than on her talent as a performer: Were those objects the best ones to choose? How could her choices have been made clearer or more effective?

| ***What to do*** In order to introduce actors to the concept of using objects to express meaning, start with a clear plastic cup of water.[4] As the actors sit in a circle, put the cup on the floor in the center of the group and ask if it communicates any meaning to them. Don't expect much of an answer. There may be a little blankness, some confusion, and a few shrugs. Someone may suggest that it would make a mess if it fell over.

Tell them you're going to add another element. Set the cup in the middle of a table where they can all see it. Ask, "Does it have any meaning now? Does it communicate anything?" Obviously there is still no particular meaning there. Then, as you're talking, describing how you're trying to find ways to make objects communicate meaning, casually scoot the cup to the edge of the table and then partially over the edge, on the verge of falling off. The dramatic tension in the room will rise. Feign surprise. "What is it?" you can ask them, the cup still teetering on the precipice of the table. When they acknowledge the feeling of tension that is being produced, point out that these are still the same two objects you had just a minute ago. The cup of water by itself didn't communicate much. When you added the table it didn't communicate anything special. But when they were put together in a certain way, all of sudden, they communicate something!

Tell them you'd like to add another element and ask one of the smaller or younger actors to join the demonstration. Have him sit on the floor directly below the cup of water so that, if it fell, he'd get wet. The thrill and delight of the group will reach new heights. "Ah! So by adding another element in a certain way, there's even more tension."

Now tell them you'd like to change things around and substitute the sitting actor with a pillow. The cup and the table and the pillow will clearly be less exciting than the cup and the table and the actor. "So," you can clarify, "not any element will do, we have to choose just the right thing. Let's try something else."

Remove the cup from the table and help the young actor stand on the table's edge. Now take away the pillow and put the cup of water on the floor where he was sitting a moment before. If he or someone else in the group doesn't spontaneously seize upon the idea, encourage him to put his hands together as if he's about to dive into the cup. You can count on there being a good laugh from the group as he readies himself for a high dive into a little cup of water. "Ah hah! It's the same three things: the cup, the table, and the actor. But before it created dramatic tension. Now it's funny. Now it's a comedy routine. So position is very important in communicating meaning." Help the actor off the table, thank him for his assistance, and let him return to the group.

Ask the group to consider the cup of water and the table. "What qualities do they have that we were able to make use of? The cup on the edge had the quality of risk. It got your attention because there was a risk that my little demonstration might go wrong and the cup would tip over and spill water on the floor. That made it interesting. Putting a pillow below the cup didn't make much of a difference, but when a person sat there the risk increased and it became more interesting. Do you think your reaction would be any different if someone you didn't like were sitting below the cup?"

For the next demonstration, pull out a balloon. As you blow it up, stop between breaths to ask what its qualities are. The cup of water had risk or danger; the table had height. What does the balloon have to offer? Follow their lead in trying things out, either demonstrating their suggestions yourself or handing one of them a balloon to demonstrate for the others. A balloon is full of expressive potential. If you continue to blow it up, shielding your face a little with your hands, there is the anxious anticipation of overinflation and explosion. It's funny when you release it and it flies around the room. Blow up another one. There is the sound of the squeal when the air is let out through a pinched nozzle; the threat of a pushpin held in close proximity; the image of defeat and exhaustion when it slowly collapses and goes limp; the potential to vigorously spring back to life again.

Put the balloon away and pull out a couple of wooden blocks. Ask for thoughts about their qualities. Since they are hard, they can be dangerous; when clapped together they can create sounds both loud and soft, harsh and gentle; they can support weight.

A beautiful and delicate piece of patterned gift wrap tissue has the quality of fragility. After first presenting it to them reverently, shock them by abruptly ripping it in two and wadding it up. Talk about what it has to offer that differentiates it from other objects. Unlike the quality of the balloon, it cannot easily return to its former shape. Once it is crushed, it can never be quite the same again. Solicit suggestions for examples of other objects in that category, perhaps an egg, especially one that has been decorated.

Simple musical instruments such as finger cymbals, a triangle, bongo drums, a rain stick, or a kalimba (African thumb piano) offer aural possibilities. In addition to the expressiveness produced by each instrument's particular sound, the actors can vary tempo, volume, and pitch to change the effect of the sound. One of the obvious qualities of sound is its potential to suddenly cease or to be interrupted by something else. Silence in the midst of sound can be as effective and expressive as the sound itself.

Pull out a couple of circular objects of different diameters, say an embroidery hoop and a hula hoop. When the embroidery hoop is held above the head, it generates an obvious image: an angel's halo. But if you then substitute the hula hoop, it can become funny: an angel who must be very, very good indeed to have such an incredibly oversized halo! The actors start to develop an appreciation for creating comedy. They start to understand how contrasts or unexpected twists can be used to make something funny. They start to see how they can consciously select and manipulate objects to help make a comic scene.

After considering a range of these or other objects and instruments, pull out a piece of fabric. Warn them that fabric is tricky, because there is a great temptation to use it as a costume or as clothing to create a character. You might demonstrate the old lady with her shawl or the vampire with his cloak. Tell them there will be time for creating characters later but, in this exercise, the task is to investigate only what qualities one piece of fabric offers that other fabrics or other objects do not. Is there something about this particular fabric that can help suggest a relationship or a mood? What are its qualities? Chinese silk has loft; it floats in the air. A piece of stage curtain is heavy and burdensome to carry. Muslin can support weight. An actor can evoke a relationship or a mood just in the way she holds it or carries it or throws it. What that actor can create with a piece of flashy red satin would be very different if she were to use a tattered piece of old burlap.

Now it is their turn.

| *What to do* Open up the box of items you've collected and spread them all out on a table or the floor. Remind the actors that they should think of all these things as tools.

When the exercise begins, the task will be for each person to pick out one or two of the tools from the pile and use them to show what something is like. They will have a few minutes to investigate the tools, to figure out how to let the tools help them communicate something about a relationship, a mood, a place, or an attitude. You may choose to have the actors work either with partners or alone. Limiting their choices at first to only one or two tools at a time will encourage simplicity. Emphasize the following points:

- It is very important to treat these tools with care and to take care of your safety and the safety of those around you.
- Each of these tools has different qualities. You may choose to start out with an idea of something you want to communicate and find a tool that will help you.
- If you don't have a particular idea to start with, find a tool that looks interesting to you and take a few minutes to see what qualities it has to offer that others don't. Look at it. Move it around. What does it make you think of? Is there some meaning that it communicates to you all by itself? Is there a second tool you can combine it with that will help show even more clearly what something is like?
- Don't rely on words—you don't need to talk at all. We're not looking for stories; the task is just to communicate some meaning. It doesn't have to be long or complicated; it can be very simple.

It is important for the actors to find the difference between declaring that an object represents something and searching to discover an evocative image. If an actor arbitrarily proclaims, "This cloth represents power and this bottle represents a person," those in the audience may or may not get it. If they do, it will probably seem contrived, an intellectual statement. It is a real challenge in this exercise to avoid obvious and sometimes heavy-handed symbolism in favor of a simpler, more elegant image. Encourage the actors always to return to the specific qualities of the object they've selected. What does it have to offer? What does it suggest to them? When they tap into an image that communicates, they'll know it. When an image is on target it will usually prompt an emphatic reaction from the rest of the group.

I remember once watching a pair of young actors as they picked through the tools. They were searching for something to help them show their sense of how fear and mistrust between people of different races is made worse by segregation. They found a small wooden louvered window shutter among the pile of found objects. For their presentation, the Caucasian girl simply held the shutter up to her face and peered anxiously through the slats at the African American boy. He looked back at her with an attitude of disgust, showing the frustration of someone who is always being prejudged. There were no characters as such; there was no story. It was basically a tableau. The rest of the group, though, sat transfixed as we saw them use that single small object to help them capture a remarkably visceral representation of a fairly complex social dynamic.

Have everyone take a few minutes to work something up and then gather together again to have them present what they've made to the rest of the group. Always be sure to thank the actors after they've shown something and give them a brief compliment. They are taking risks, venturing into unknown territory, and a little positive encouragement goes a long way.

Giving Feedback

Appropriately framing the critiques of the presentations is very important. Don't expect polished work; these are experiments and some will fail. Others will be astonishing. The only real concern is: What did you see the actor(s) do? What was communicated by what they did?

| ***What to do*** After each performer or pair of performers makes a presentation, ask the others to describe what they saw, what they got from it. Ask them to avoid attempts to derive a story from what they saw. Keep the focus on the kind of feeling the presentation produced or what it made the spectators think of.

Once the spectators have had an opportunity to make their reports, ask the performers what they were trying to get across. The group can then consider whether the presentation was a success or whether there were details that could be emphasized or altered to make it clearer or more evocative. In some cases, there may be just one little aspect of the presentation that gives a flash of inspiration. Direct attention to that. Encourage comment about whatever specific things the actors did that made an impact on the audience. After everyone has shown his work, the actors can try another round with something fresh or they can choose to work in some adjustments to their previous piece.

Investigations Without Tools

| ***What to do*** As the actors become more comfortable with the exercise, you can challenge them to try it without the use of the props or objects, fabric or instruments. They can try to create meaning vocally with shouts, snarls, whistles, laughter, whispers, screams, other vocalized sound effects, or even a single word. They can try to create meaning with the use of ges-

ture, movement, or physical relationship between actors, making use of differences or similarities in size, age, gender, and so on. Working with their bodies alone will tempt them to create whole pantomimed characters. Discourage this. The task remains: How can a simple sound or gesture or physical movement/attitude be used to reveal meaning?

As described previously, the actors can continue to investigate the tools as a warm-up exercise throughout the script development process. As they improve their ability to craft random images that evoke meaning, they can begin to apply their skill to creating a scene. When they turn their attention to the issues in their play and start to identify the social dynamics of a specific situation, they'll be prepared. They'll be able to use their bodies, their voices, and their tools to translate what happened into powerful stage pictures that communicate what they see to their audience.

2 IDENTIFYING AND INVESTIGATING THE TOPIC

Until we take action together, to understand, to deal with the given problem that we share in common, neither of us has the knowledge that's required to solve that problem. The knowledge itself is the product of our action.
John O'Neal

CHOOSING A TOPIC

Your cast members may already have a topic in mind. Perhaps they are all passionately concerned about the environment or about drug and alcohol abuse. They want to use theatre to call attention to the problem and have asked you to assist them. Or perhaps a recent significant event such as the suicide of a fellow student or a violent confrontation at school has drawn them together. To try to better understand what happened and to shed some light on the situation and its aftermath, they have decided to make a piece of theatre and perform it for the rest of the school community. Or it could be that they are involved in some positive activity they feel doesn't receive enough recognition so they hope to put together a show that celebrates the successes they've had and the challenges they've managed to overcome.

Or, as their teacher, you may have proposed the idea to them. You know how the enthusiasm and creativity generated by putting on a show can add a dynamic sense of purpose to a group and can foster productive discussions about important issues. With that in mind, you have suggested using theatre to explore and present some issue. You might spend some time helping the group develop some of the ensemble skills described in the previous section, but before long they will need to decide what the subject of their performance will be.

| *What to do* If the group doesn't already have a topic, ask each person to write down what he or she feels are the most important issues that the group faces. You may choose to have them consider this overnight or over the course of several days. Gather the separate ideas and write them on a large sheet of paper or chalkboard. If there are multiple suggestions for the same topic, indicate how many times it has come up with check marks or ditto marks. After looking over the list, it may be obvious to the group that there is general consensus about a single theme. Even if the ideas are quite different from one another, you can challenge the group to find a unifying thread among the suggestions. For example, let's say the list includes the following:

girls being harassed by boys in the hallways
racial prejudice
no one listens to kids
skaters are treated like criminals

It's not too much of a stretch to say that the common denominator among all these concerns is the issue of how people treat one another across lines of difference: gender, race, age, and culture (skateboarding could be seen as an aspect of youth culture). Within that framework, and given enough time, it is possible to create a script addressing all the specific concerns that fall within the general category.

| ***Why*** In order for everyone to feel a sense of ownership about the project, it is important that each person shares in the decision about choice of topic. In later brainstorming sessions, the ideas will all generally be complementary, as each person contributes to the list. But submitting ideas for choosing a topic can be seen as competitive. The participants may start to wrangle over the relative merits of their personal agendas. Those with less confidence about their ideas can be drowned out in the enthusiasm. If everyone writes down his ideas and all the ideas are posted together anonymously, the less outgoing members of the group are not as likely to get lost in the fray.

Even when the ideas are all listed at once, the process of determining a topic can still lapse into factional disputes. To bypass this problem, ask everyone to consider what issues the group faces rather than just listing her own concerns. Their suggestions will still be influenced by personal experience, but phrasing it in this way encourages cast members to consider what is important both to themselves and to their community.

Effective Questioning

Write up the general topic for everyone to see. As the actors begin to examine their chosen topic, *X*, you can substantially influence the direction of the discussion by being selective about the kinds of questions you ask. For example, if you ask, "What do you think about *X*?" the response will tend to be in the form of a value judgment: "I think *X* is bad because . . ." or "*X* is good because . . ." or "I don't have an opinion about *X*." It's a start, but it doesn't go very far. It doesn't reveal much about *X* beyond personal sentiment. If you ask, "Who is responsible for *X*?" the answer will be a list, maybe a short one, of those at fault. Discussions of blame also tend not to go very far. If someone else is identified as being at fault, we feel resolved of responsibility and the discussion may turn toward feelings of rage or victimization. If we are the ones identified at fault, we may want to dispute it or feel guilty about it. Talking about those feelings may be warranted but, for the purpose of building a script, those discussions are not very productive.

However, if you ask:

How does *X* start?
What makes *X* continue?
What leads people to let *X* continue?
What gets people to do something about *X*?
What changes people's minds about *X*?
What makes people see *X* in a different way?
What stops *X* cold?
What divides people over *X*?
What unites people over *X*?

The responses all involve human interactions. By adjusting the questions, the discussion has been framed so that it leads to analysis of the social dynamic. These questions generate more questions and excite interest in further investigation. They also allow for multiple, sometimes contradictory, perspectives to be put forth side by side.

We want to go down that road. We want our actors to become passionate about considering how people behave in dealing with *X*. We want them to spend time ruminating over how relationships are affected by *X*, how different people respond to *X*. We want to stimulate our actors' desire to understand more about the specific ways in which human beings confront problems and overcome adversity, especially as it relates to *X*.[5]

| *What to do* Begin by talking to the group very directly about how different kinds of questions lead to different kinds of discussions and give examples like the ones in the previous section. ("What do you think about . . . ?" leading to value judgments such as good, bad, or I don't know; "Who is responsible . . . ?" leading to unproductive blame and anger, or guilt and arguments.) Point out that everyone has opinions about what is good or bad, but not everyone understands why different people wind up doing what they do. Write out the list of questions starting with "How does *X* start?," replacing the *X*'s with a blank line or with some appropriate aspect of the chosen topic (see Questions worksheet, p. 35). As the actors look over this list of questions, take a moment to reiterate your belief that their insight about these kinds of questions is valuable and important. Through this project they can start to understand more about the answers to these kinds of questions and, through their performance, they can share their ideas with their audience.

Working together, solicit suggestions for answers to the questions you have listed and write them up. You may choose to have cast members start with quick writes; writing down responses in their notebooks for a few minutes before everyone starts calling out their ideas. After some brainstorming, start to solicit ideas for more questions along the same lines. Challenge them to design their own questions about the topic that will lead to answers about human interactions: how the issue affects people, how different people behave in response to it.

The amount of time to spend on this stage of the work is flexible. It will vary in each group according to the scale of the project and how much time is available. If your timetable allows for it, you may want to expand the questioning phase to include research-based questions, such as:

> What else do we need to know about *X*?
> Where can we go to get more information?
> Who else would know about *X* and where will we find those people?
> Are there books, magazines, or videos with information about *X*?
> Where will we find those resources?

You or the cast members can seek out guests who have been identified as having a particular expertise on the subject under consideration and invite them to the scripting workshops or visit them for an interview, discussion, or learning activity. If there are videos, magazine articles, or books with information useful to the cast, time can be made for cast members to review them and report to the rest of the group. These resources can be viewed with the same attitude: What do they tell us about how people behave around this issue?

Why It is vital that the cast members are aware of the reasons why the discussions are being framed in this way. The more they are aware of what they are doing, the more successful they will be in attaining their goal. Fundamentally, the role of the director in this script development process is to teach cast members techniques and strategies for creating their own work. You could simply ask these questions and guide the discussion along but, by spending a moment to demonstrate that not all kinds of questions lead to the same answers, you can give the participants the means to take over the process themselves. Once they clarify what they're working toward and learn how to shape the questions that will help them get there, the work will be theirs, and they'll ultimately perform it with passion, authority, and depth.

Some Questions About ____________________

How does ____________________ start?

What makes ____________________ continue?

What leads people to let ____________________ continue?

What gets people to do something about ____________________ ?

What changes people's minds about ____________________ ?

What makes people see ____________________ in a different way?

What stops ____________________ cold?

What divides people over ____________________ ?

What unites people over ____________________ ?

What else do we need to know about ____________________ ?

Where can we go to get more information?

Who else would know about ____________________ and where will we find those people?

Are there books, magazines, or videos with information about ____________________ and where will we find those resources?

Making Topic Cards

Throughout this stage of the work, cast members mull over the specific things they want to be sure to include in their presentation. As they think up questions and respond to them, as they learn more about the topic from their research and from one another, certain aspects of the issue will filter out as particularly important to them. Now the time has come to compile their ideas.

| ***What to do*** As with the other brainstorming sessions, write down all ideas on a chalkboard or a large sheet of paper. The goal is to wind up with a list of the cast members' gut feelings about what needs to be addressed in their show or, if you're working on a smaller scale, aspects of the single idea they feel they want to present in their scene, song, or piece of choreography. These ideas do not need to be written in complete sentences; they do not even need to be fully explained or articulated. However, it is most important that they are observations and questions, rather than proclamations. For example, in a show about prejudice and diversity, one group I worked with wanted their script to deal with the following issues:

how people respond to prejudice
how a person overcomes his own prejudices
how a person deals with somebody who does or says something prejudiced
the ways that we're all connected
the good things about being different
attitudes and stereotypes between males and females
differences in religious beliefs
what America is—people, beliefs, etc.
how people react to different accents
how people react to slang
not being taken seriously
the way that problems get worse when people who disagree don't stop to listen to each other

We invited a guest to our scripting workshops to lead a session about unlearning racism. During the discussion, the concept of being an ally came up. There was much conversation about what an ally is compared to what a friend is and how the two are related. As we continued to develop our list, that new concern surfaced:

what it means to be an ally
how an ally is similar or different from a friend

In that same session, the group talked about how people respond differently to stereotypes being leveled at them. That discussion clearly led to a few more suggestions:

why some people believe the stereotypes about themselves and let it get them down

why some people believe the stereotypes about themselves and try so hard to prove to others that they're not like the stereotype
why some people don't believe the stereotypes and know that they're okay the way they are
why no one is beyond being stereotyped

Note that in these examples, the cast avoided proclamations aimed at teaching or preaching such as "Prejudice is bad," or "People should treat each other better." If they start out with a proclamation, they will be inclined to create material designed to prove the point, to convince an audience of the truth of the statement. Alternatively, if they begin with an observation or question, they will be drawn toward clarifying it in their script, exploring it in depth.

After everyone has had a say, take a moment to review each item and make sure that everybody more or less understands the meaning or intent of each one. The phrasing of some ideas might be a little ephemeral and it is important that no one feels mystified or left out. Some ideas might be grouped together as variations on a similar thought. Others might be clarified, even slightly reworded, after discussion.

The next step for the cast or the director is to transfer items from the large unwieldy list onto individual Topic Cards; four-by-six-inch cards work well. Topic Cards can be neatly hand lettered or printed in a large, bold typeface. When the cards are ready, thumbtack each one to a bulletin board—the idea board—for everyone to see.

| *Why* The board will play a central part in the work ahead. These initial gut impressions and concerns, each on a separate card, will serve as catalysts for the actors to bring to mind representative stories to share. Holding a card in his hand, an actor will tell not just any story, but an anecdote about something that has to do with what's on that card. When he's finished, the story will be *unpacked*: all the listeners will identify and list whatever details struck them as significant. Then the next actor will tell an anecdote that also relates to what's on the card. When she's done, her story will be unpacked by the rest of the group. The stories they tell may be wildly different, but the Topic Cards help the actors target experiences that have a common link. As the actors listen to story after story, they'll gradually gain an appreciation for how these kinds of situations play out: the attitudes, the choices that people tend to make, the way the relationships work, and the general patterns of behavior.

The stories the actors tell do not have to be based on personal experiences. I have had groups unpack stories read aloud from magazine and newspaper articles, as well as stories told by invited visitors and stories heard on video programs. Whether the story comes from a cast member's own testimonial or via research, the process is the same: listening to how it resonates and interpreting what it reveals.

Recalling a Story and Unpacking It: Gests

| *What to do* Tell the group that in a few minutes you're going to ask for a volunteer to pick one of the cards. She will tell the rest of the group about something that happened to her or something she saw that has to do with what's on that card. Everyone else's job will be to listen. Explain how, after listening to a story, it is hard to remember the whole thing word for word, but certain things will stand out. There may be one or two things in the story that really got them as they listened. It may have been what one person said or did that stands out, or it could even be a sound that was described. Sometimes these things are memorable because they are surprising or shocking. Sometimes it is because they are so typical of what happens in similar situations—they are what people always seem to say or do or hear.

Here are some examples to illustrate this idea, which you may put into your own words or use as a starting place to make up your own:

What People Say

In a story about being picked on, the thing that stands out might be when someone in the story slowly said, "You . . . are . . . *worthless!*"

In a story about friends, the one sentence or phrase that stands out could be "The best times I ever had were with those guys." That one line sums up the whole story.

Gestures with Arms or Hands

In a story about gossip and rumors, the storyteller may describe how someone suddenly covered her mouth as she realized that her gossip involved a friend standing next to her. That one little gesture of the hand going up—oops—says a lot about how gossip works. It shows that we do it even though we know it can hurt people and how easy it is to get out of control.

Maybe there's a story about a guy having to deal with a bully who's threatened to beat him up after school. The bully comes up behind this guy and puts his hand on the guy's shoulder. That single gesture of the hand coming down says a lot about the whole situation of feeling trapped. In a different story, the exact same gesture could sum up the opposite feeling. There could be a story about someone who felt isolated and completely rejected by everybody. Just when things were getting as bad as they could get, someone put a hand on his shoulder and told him that he's not alone. An important part of the whole story is summed up by that one gesture and the few words he said.[6]

In a story about how people deal with being upset, the thing that stands out could be the gesture of a girl hiding in her room and stuffing candy bars into her mouth.

A gesture could be suddenly grabbing a phone and dialing after you've been staring at it for five minutes, figuring out what to say and working up the courage to call.

A Gesture Doesn't Have to Be Just the Movement of Hands or Arms

A gesture could be the way somebody looks at you that stops you in your tracks, or the way somebody avoids looking at you when he's afraid, lying, or in pain. It could be somebody spitting at a person, or the look on the face of someone who is trying desperately not to cry. It could be busting through the ribbon at the finish line of a race. These are gestures, too, because they involve some physical action. In each case, they are the things that might stand out in a story.

Sounds

It can also be a sound that really sums things up. The sound of whispering might stand out in a story about a person who was too ashamed or too scared to talk out loud about what was happening to her. In a different story, it could be the sound of a crowd cheering or a gunshot that stays in your memory. Maybe it's the sound of no sound if, in a story about fear, someone described being called on to give an answer in class and there was complete silence while everyone stared and waited.

Explain to the cast that there is a word for this. It's called a *gest* (pronounced "jest"). It is a translation of the German word *gestus* (pronounced "guest-oos"), which is a combination of *gist*, as in the gist of what's happening, and *gesture*, as in what somebody does or says. It's an actual, physical thing in the story that says it all about what was happening right then. The great thing about a gest is that it has a lot of power. One simple gest can communicate a lot all by itself. It's possible to pick it out of a story and put it into your script to help audience members understand in their guts what something was like for the people who were there. Just as gests grab you when you're listening to the story, they can grab members of an audience when they're watching a performance.[7]

Now ask for your volunteer. Ask her to pick out a card that relates to an experience she's had or something she's seen. Ask her to tell what happened: who was there, what was going on, what people said, and what they did. The volunteer can describe both what she was thinking at the time and what stands out for her now, looking back on it. Most importantly, though, her job is to get all the listeners to really understand what the experience was like in whatever way she can. Remind the rest of the participants that the stories people tell here are to be kept in confidence, they are not to be shared with anyone outside the group.

These are some of the gests participants should listen for as the volunteer tells her story:

the phrases, words, or sentences that stand out
the physical things in the story that stand out
the sounds that stand out

The first volunteer now tells her story. When she finishes, it is the group's turn to unpack it. They should write up the gests on a large sheet in the three categories: "phrases," "gestures," and "sounds." You may choose to add a fourth category, "other," for things that stand out but don't fit into any of the other categories. As the group gathers impressions, there may be contradictions. Different people may find different aspects of the event significant. That is valuable. Keep note of them all.

| *Why* The notion of using gests in theatre comes from the German playwright, director, and poet Bertolt Brecht. The idea that an individual or group can look for and identify a gest has multiple implications. To begin with, it gives the observers something specific to hunt for. And it is usually an enthusiastic hunt. Compared to a discussion format, actors zeroing in on gests aren't as limited by lack of articulation skills due to age, cultural difference, level of education, or insufficient mastery of a second language. They translate their understanding of a situation's underlying dynamic directly into theatrical terms.

Disputes over choices of a gest only serve to continually clarify the actors' understanding of the issue. They hold up a possible gest for inspection and pitch ideas about how to adjust or refine it until it is stronger and more accurate. Their work may lead to a series of separate gests as they start to discern subtle differences. Contradictions reveal that what may be most significant to one is only a passing detail to another. Both are valuable. Together they show contrasts in perception and experience.

Brecht distinguished between ordinary gests and social gests. He observed that it is a common tendency of art to remove the social element in any gest, to use the power of an image without reference to its context. This is certainly true in television (e.g., music videos). A big knife can be a violent image, but it doesn't reveal anything about violence. To make it a social gest, it must be put into context. Rather than just showing pain, one can show pain as the result of a specific circumstance.[8]

For now, however, the actors are just gathering evocative images, ordinary gests. That is perfectly all right. When the time comes for them to begin to select gests from their list and integrate them into their script, you can encourage them to become conscientious about the way they are using the gests. Are they using them for shock value or to contribute to the audience's understanding of the character's behavior?

Recalling a Story and Unpacking It: Tropes[9]

The next step in unpacking the story calls for considering some nonliteral comparisons. In order to clarify their understanding of what happened, the actors will imagine what else this situation is like (similes) and what it is not like (opposites); they will expand what happened into comic proportions (comedy version) and they will contract it down into the single most important thing that sums it all up (the two-second or scaled-down version); finally, they will leave words and images behind and find the sound equivalent of the social interaction (musical or rhythmic version).

What Else Is It Like (Similes)?

| ***What to do*** Ask the cast members to think about what happened in the story and to use their imaginations to come up with similes describing what the situation was like. It can be anything at all, but the challenge is to find a simile that truly captures the spirit of what was happening. For example: A teacher overreacting to an obstinate student *is like a person yelling at a car engine that won't start.* A girl who plays dumb so that boys will like her more *is like someone who puts tape across her own mouth.* A group of out of control kids *is like a fire that gets out of hand.* A murdered child *is like a candle put out by a hammer.*

| **Why** The question "What else is it like?" opens the floodgates of the imagination. This exercise starts the process of stripping away the realistic details of a story in order to make a bold interpretation of the social dynamic that lies behind the story. During the brainstorming session, certain similes may be way off base. List them anyway. Trust that, through the course of the exercise, the cast members will be able to choose and refine those images that are right on target.

What Is the Big, Exaggerated, or Comedy Version?

| ***What to do*** Explain that another way to get to the heart of what happened is to expand what people did into comic proportions. Ask the group to exaggerate what happened in the story until it becomes funny. For example, protective parents disapproving of their daughter's new boyfriend might become tough cops giving him the third degree in an interrogation cell. Or, if they insisted on chaperoning the date, the cast might imagine the parents riding piggyback on the teenagers, looking over their shoulders. Or, shown from the parents' perspective, maybe the daughter chides them and pleads with them to accept her choice of a boyfriend, who is literally a great hulking, drooling, snarling beast.

It will be tempting for some participants to make a story funny simply by changing one of the elements or introducing a wacky twist. That may make everyone laugh, but it won't clarify what happened. Encourage them to be diligent about finding humor by exaggerating what really happened, not by changing or adding something in order to make a joke.

| **Why** Part of the rationale for this exercise is simply to find a humorous way of seeing one's life experiences. Characterizing what happened as a comedy can allow the actors to step back from their emotional responses to a situation. But it involves more than just being able to laugh at oneself. Once again, playing with the boundaries of literal reality encourages cast members to define the essential social relationships and choices being made within a story. The details about an interaction that make it funny can be very telling. They are often the same details that define the nature of the relationship.

What Is the Opposite of It?

| ***What to do*** Ask cast members to describe what the opposite of this situation would be. Once they have identified the opposite, have them consider what they believe happened that made things turn out the way they did, rather than the opposite way.

| ***Why*** Once cast members define the opposite of a situation, they can begin to focus on why it didn't turn out that way. In other words, by imagining *what* it is not, one can start to consider *why* it is not. The question can sometimes reveal unexpected dimensions. For example, in the illustration of protective parents given previously, the actors may propose that the opposite of what happened would be parents who trust their daughter's judgment about boyfriends. The question of opposites clarifies for them that the issue is not, as it first appeared to be, about overprotection. The situation hinges on trust; that's what would be different. When they begin to ask what happened to make it turn out this way, the cast starts to look beyond the frame of the story and to assemble the history of events that culminated in the experience as described. Why don't the parents trust their daughter? Had the parents' trust been abused in the past? If so, at what point? Or is the mistrust unwarranted? Was trust established and then the rules changed? Why? All these questions lead to a clearer understanding of the situation.

What Is the Two-Second Version?

| ***What to do*** Ask cast members to find the one thing that can show what happened in the story, or the most important part of what happened, in no more than two seconds. They must identify the one or two words, the one gesture or movement or look that says it all.

In a variation of the two-second version, they can imagine the scaled-down version. If the story were about a home burning down, it might be imagined in a scaled-down version as a single match being struck. An assault might be scaled down to a single movement and fearful cry.

| ***Why*** Like the exercise with similies, this is another way to force the cast members to define an incident precisely—and dramatically. It brings the essential elements of the experience to the surface.

What Is the Rhythmic or Musical Version?

| ***What to do*** Finally, ask the actors to translate the essence of what happened into musical or rhythmic terms. Ask them to demonstrate the sense of what happened as if they had to explain it with sound to someone who didn't speak their language. The goal is to create the equivalent, in sound, of what happened in the story. It can be percussive, with woodblocks or fingers drumming on something, or vocalized like scat singing. It can be hummed or whistled, or an instrument can be used such as a kazoo, a slide whistle, a tambourine, a kalimba, or a bell. They can communicate what happened by changing volume, tempo, or pitch or by using interrup-

tions or pauses. For example, a story about a fun time that was suddenly interrupted could easily be translated into sound. Or a story about two very different people enjoying each other's company could be characterized by a powerful bass sound and a playful soprano. The musical dynamic could illustrate the social dynamic. What happened between those two people could be shown in the way the two sounds play in counterpoint, including how the exchange started, what happened next, and how it resolved.

| ***Why*** This is just one more way to define what happened by stepping away from the literal. As the cast has run the story through one exercise after another, the particulars of this story have become unimportant. It is no longer about one person's experience. The details have been peeled away and the cast has arrived at the heart of the social dynamics in terms that are vivid and expressive—in a word, theatrical.

Along with the gests collected earlier, write up each of these ideas on the large sheet according to category:

What else is it like?
The opposite of what happened would be . . .
The big, exaggerated, or comedy version of what happened would be . . .
The two-second or scaled-down version of what happened would be . . .
The musical or rhythmic version of what happened would be . . .
(This can be notated as best as possible on paper or tape-recorded.)

Now review what the group has collected. The actors have finished unpacking their first story. Other cast members will also have stories to tell about experiences with the issue on that first Topic Card. You may choose to ask a few more volunteers to tell their stories to the whole group and unpack them together. Or, if you feel they have got the hang of it, they can separate into smaller groups at this point.

When you're ready, divide the cast into small groups of five or six people. Working in their small groups, they take turns telling stories about experiences related to what's on the card they have chosen. After the story is told, the others unpack it. To help keep the actors focused, I've found it useful to provide them with an Unpacking List with all the appropriate questions (see worksheet, p. 44). As they unpack stories, cast members should not feel it is necessary to come up with responses to each and every question. Some questions may not trigger any response at all; others may spark dozens of ideas. After the first story is unpacked, the next person can either tell a story related to the Topic Card, or choose to pass, and the process is repeated. When all are finished with one Topic Card, the whole group meets again and the smaller groups report on their findings.

Unpacking List

This will be a piece about:

Tell a story about it. It can be something you were involved in, something you saw or something you read about. The listeners should think about what stands out in the story.

Phrases (what people said)

What phrases stood out?

Gestures (what people did)

What were the physical things in the story that stood out?

Sounds

What sounds stood out?

What else is it like (similes)?

The comedy version of what happened would be:

The opposite of what happened would be:

Also, what do you think made it turn out the way it did and not the opposite way?

The two-second or scaled-down version of what happened would be:

The rhythmic or musical version of what happened would be:

(Translate what happened into music or rhythm as if you're explaining it to someone who doesn't understand your language.)

Is there anything else that stands out in this story?

Clarifying the Sequence of What Happens

The cast members have now unpacked a series of stories inspired by one Topic Card. They've singled out evocative phrases, gestures, and sounds as well as imaginative tropes that characterize what happened. They will be able to use this raw material when they start to assemble the text and stage directions of their script, the lyrics of their songs, or their choreography. But the process of identifying all these elements has another important purpose. As the actors strip away the details and compare what is striking among related anecdotes, it gradually becomes clear to them that each of their separate stories have things in common. Despite outward differences, there may be four stories in which the individuals all behaved in the same way. What they said or did was pretty much the same as what their counterparts said or did. In all four cases, there were similarities in the gests and tropes. In all four cases, behaviors and the outcome of actions were more or less the same. Now there may be a fifth story that started out the same way, but at some point veered off from the others and ended up differently. That's what the actors are looking for: those patterns and variations that reveal what our experiences have in common and where they diverge. Once they've identified these personal and social dynamics, they are equipped to design an original piece of theatre about the behavior itself, in all its complexity, not just an illustration of one particular story.

It can still be difficult, though, for the actors to make connections across stories, to separate the elements from the plot. To help them along, you can ask them to review their stories according to what people *did*.

| ***What to do*** Begin by asking the group to look over the Unpacking List for each story. For each of the phrases, gestures, sounds, or other details the actors have compiled, ask the following questions:

What was that person trying to do?
Did it change anything? If so, how did it change?
What happened next?

For example:

What was she trying to do?
When she reached up and took off her earrings, she was showing she was serious about fighting.

Did it change anything? How?
The other girl saw that she wasn't going to back off.

What happened next?
The other girl started looking around for a way out.

In this example, what two girls in conflict did was noted during the unpacking as a gesture of removing earrings and a gesture of looking for an escape route. In another story, the threat and response may be in the form of a phrase or a sound. As the performers move from one Unpacking List to the next, their sense of the common denominators among all the stories will become more and more clear. The sequence of what people did, the similarities and differences, will become more important than the details of each story. The group may want to add more similies, comedy versions, two-second versions, or rhythmic versions at this point.

| *Why* Clarifying what people did in the stories sheds light on the ways in which one action influenced the next. This is a critical step toward developing perceptions about when and how and why choices are made—where the turning points are. That is the foundation for the actors' understanding of what they want to communicate in their scenes.

The idea that one can make sense of how different stories relate to one another according to what the characters do is not a new one. In the late 1920s, Vladimir Propp's *Morphology of the Folktale* reinvented the way that folklorists looked at traditional tales. Propp was responding to what he felt was the haphazard way that Russian folktales had historically been categorized. Scholars agreed that in order to study folktales as a whole, the stories must first be organized and classified. But Propp believed that existing divisions were misleading. Tales were commonly lumped together because they happened to share a particular character, such as all the stories about Baba Yaga, or share character types, such as all the stories about three brothers or all the stories about wise maidens. Folktales that contained elements of fantasy were considered apart from those about everyday life. Both were distinguished from stories about animals.

The problem was that these classifications often overlapped. If a story included animals, a witch, and a fight with a dragon, to which category would it belong? If the fight scenes were particularly striking, the other elements could be arbitrarily dismissed and the tale cataloged as a story about a dragon fight. These classifications also failed to reveal authentic patterns and relationships between tales. Propp recognized that a tale in which a dragon counsels a young prince should not be automatically compared to other tales about dragons; it should be compared to tales about counselors. By looking at what the characters did regardless of who they were, he argued that one could see through the colorful clutter of narrative details and begin to spot recurrent patterns and variations among seemingly dissimilar tales.[10] This same approach allows actors to spot patterns and variations in the stories they tell.

This section has been all about finding links between stories. Recounting first- and second-hand experiences, the actors have gathered the phrases, gestures, sounds, and analogous versions of events that define the core of each story they've told. Sifting out these elements has enabled them to compare and contrast multiple stories on the same topic. After clarifying the progression of actions in each story, they've found parallels and variations revealing patterns of behavior that, for them, characterize the nature of relationships in certain circumstances.

The actors have stripped these stories down to their fundamental elements. The material they have gathered, though, is all relatively static. They have put together a collection of moments that are evocative, but brief. Now, to make theatre that is fluid, textured, and multidimensional, they'll want to build them up again, to layer these dramatic and comic moments with imagery and text that will help expand and illuminate what they've decided to show their audience.

Gathering More Material

The cast has spent some time analyzing and comparing their stories. The actors have discovered some patterns of responses to events that all these stories have in common, and they've clarified the ways in which people's choices vary. At this point they can look back at the whole progression of important moments and give a little creative attention to each step along the way.

| *What to do* After first reviewing all the material the group has gathered on a particular Topic Card, have cast members break into smaller groups to spend a little time coming up with some additional existing material that reflects the dynamic of each step (see Gathering More Material worksheet, p. 50). For example, let's say a few actors are looking at a moment in which a person becomes involved with something against his better judgment. They have identified the fear of looking foolish, that feeling of being under pressure to rise to the challenge of a dare. They ask themselves, their friends, and librarians what other images, fictional characters, historical characters, rhymes, and pictures or text from magazines capture the spirit or quality of that feeling. They ask themselves what else is in this category and who else has been in this situation.

For example, someone who has spent time on a playground skipping rope might suggest the old jump rope rhyme:

> Policeman, policeman, do your duty,
> Here comes ______
> And she's a cutie;
> She can jump, she can twist,
> But I bet she can't do this.

Or the actors might put together a list of phrases they associate with dares:

> What are you, chicken?
> Hey, I've been doing this for years and I've never had a problem.
> What's the matter, can't you handle it?
> We're just having a little fun, get over it!

They could come up with a list of other people in the category who are afraid of looking weak in front of others: a gangster being ordered to make his first hit; a rookie ballplayer stepping up to the plate for the first time in the major leagues. (Educator Dorothy Heathcote would say, "Who else is in the *brotherhood* of those afraid of looking weak in front of others?")

One actor might make a trip to the library to ask the librarian's advice for ideas about scenes from books or stories that involve someone going along with the crowd because he didn't want to look uncool. The librarian thinks for a moment and suggests the scene in Carlo Collodi's *Pinocchio* in which Pinocchio decides to go with Lampwick and the other boys on the donkey cart even though, at first, he doesn't think it's such a good idea. The actor checks out the book and takes a look. Some actors may return to the Unpacking List to come up with more gests, similes, and comedy, two-second, or rhythmic versions related to the experience they are investigating. Finally, some actors might root through the tools to find a way to capture the specific sense of this tough situation through physical imagery using props, fabric, or musical instruments.

When the cast members are ready, have them select new cards and unpack more stories. They continue this process, generating more material for each step in the progression. By the time they've finished this stage of script development, the actors have at their disposal baskets full of raw material with which to fashion scenes, songs, choreography, and staging. They've handpicked the elements that, for them, resonate with accuracy some of the truths about human behavior and human relationships. Next they get to the fun part: weaving it all together into their performance pieces.

Gathering More Material

Now that you have a better understanding of what happens in a situation like this, think about the following questions. Discuss them with others in the group. Talk to your friends, your family, librarians, teachers, or anyone else who might have some ideas.

Who else in books or stories or in the history of the world has ever been in a situation like this, and what did they do?

Has a situation like this ever been in

a rhyme?
a song?
a poem?
a painting or a drawing?
a photograph?

Write down more phrases, gestures, or sounds; similes, comedy versions, two-second versions, or rhythmic versions of what happens in a situation like this, now that you understand it better.

Use the tools—props, fabric, or musical instruments—to find a way that explains what happens in a situation like this, now that you understand it better.

3 BUILDING DIALOGUE, LYRICS, AND CHOREOGRAPHY

Theatre to me is the physical word, the ability to center the word in a physical context, to root the word, the concept, in astonishing visual, musical, and physical actions.
James Schevill

What should we call the segments in the show that are about to become either dramatic or comic scenes, songs, choreography, and transitions? Skits? Scenes? Sketches? Consider using the word *piece* to describe a segment in development. *Piece* is a purposefully vague term. It is useful because, as a script is being put together, a piece dealing with one aspect of the theme can be developed in any direction. It may eventually wind up being a monologue, a scene with dialogue, a solo song, a duet, a choral number, movement, some combination thereof, or something else altogether. The term doesn't tie it down conceptually from the start. The director can say, "Let's work on this piece about ______," and the cast is open to the possibility that the idea could take any number of forms. If it doesn't work one way, as song lyrics for example, the group can recast the idea as a scene or as dance until a form is found that succeeds.

POTENTIAL FORMS

The performance pieces will take a variety of basic forms including, but not limited to:

- scenes revealing a relationship between actors relying on dialogue, gesture, or physical interplay of some kind
- monologues
    - soliloquy style—a character working out a problem aloud
    - testimonial style—a character describing an experience
- songs
    - solos
    - duets

trios

songs with multiple voices or musical choruses

- spoken choruses
- choreography

There are no limits to the combination of forms that can be incorporated into a single performance piece. A piece may include layers of lyrical language and realistic speech. It may include stylized physical action, choreography, and natural-looking blocking. In a scene with spoken words, the character's feeling may reach a level at which it can no longer be contained in speech so she suddenly begins to sing or dance. This is, of course, the standard practice in conventional musical theatre. Voices and musical instruments can underscore a mood, or realistic sounds can evoke an environment.

The structure of each piece will have a beginning, a middle, and an end. The actors will design each piece to reflect what they have learned about the nature of a certain type of situation and they may emphasize the turning points—how and why the situation changes. Inspiration for the structure of a piece may come from any of the categories on the list: a simile, the comedy version, the opposite, or even the musical or rhythmic version. The cast may borrow the beginning, middle, and end of a story they've identified through some analogous cultural, historical, or fictional material they have gathered. In some cases, the perfect structure will be obvious to everyone. In other cases, it will require some experimentation.

BUILDING THE PIECES

What is the first step? A director and cast can often find clues about where to start on any given piece by examining the makeup of the elements they've put on their Unpacking Lists. The lists rarely have an even distribution of material; look for questions that have inspired the most potent responses.

As a very general rule of thumb:

- Lists featuring particularly well-founded similes or striking links to analogous stories/characters lend themselves either to scenes that involve interaction between actors or to monologues.
- Lists full of phrases that get to the heart of an issue can be used for dialogue or even lyrical spoken text, but vivid phrases also lend themselves well to song lyrics.
- A series of evocative gestures will often serve as the foundation for choreography.

With this in mind, review the list to see if a starting place suggests itself. You will be surprised at how these pieces seem to spring into form, albeit roughly hewn form, when you simply look at the elements that have been laid out. That, in a nutshell, is the aim of all the preparatory work. Once the actors have compiled an assortment of vividly expressive ingredients, the recipe for assembling them into a coherent form is often self-evident. If it doesn't fit one way, recombine the elements in another way. Find what works. If the basic form of the piece seems effective but ragged, it can always be refined and polished in rehearsal.

Again, keep in mind that these pieces will not fit into neat categories. The clues provide a starting place, but the very range of elements allows the cast members to communicate what they see on many levels at once. A single image about the loss of a parent, developed while investigating the tools, might have involved tenderly holding an old dress. If a song were developed around that topic, the staging might include someone singing to the dress while holding it. On an entirely different song, the actors may find ideas for a melody by looking over the similes they've chosen. "She treats them like she's a drum majorette and they're the marching band" might lead them to borrow a tune from Sousa; if it were suggested that "it's like a funeral," they might make their song follow the rhythm and form of a Kaddish. Or the song may incorporate spoken text and sound effects, blurring the division between song and scene. All these layers will help them theatrically reveal different aspects of the situation being examined.

Sample One: Song Lyrics

In one group I worked with, stories were unpacked based on a Topic Card that read, "the way that problems get worse when people who disagree don't stop to listen to each other." An actor described a disastrous day at her school when students tried to let their feelings about a divisive issue be known in a peaceful way. They were deferred, denied, and then forcibly silenced. Their resentment turned to rage and they lost control. Finally, several students, having been locked in a classroom, smashed through a window. The way in which frustration and anger turns to a physical lashing out was captured in that single gesture of breaking glass. That actor's story was followed by someone else's story on the same topic. In the second story, the reaction to being outshouted was characterized by a very different gesture. The second storyteller described someone who buried her face in her hands, defeated.

The group gathered additional material, including a large list of similes. By the end of the process, we found the material for this piece was heavily weighted in favor of significant phrases:

No, I'm not gonna be quiet.
Stop acting stupid.
It's nothing—you kids are just being childish.
You're just kids—I don't want to talk about it—I don't want to talk to you.
I think I'm right (I think it's right).
I can't take this anymore.
You're pushing me aside.
I'm in control—No, I'm in control.

I'm tired of being ignored.
I want an equal voice.
Can't you hear what I'm saying?
Now you have to hear me!
Can't we work it out?
We're not going to change our minds about it.
Listen to me!
Just stop!

Following our general rule of thumb, the large number of phrases led us to consider making a song. The phrases seemed to fall into three categories representing three specific points of view: the one who feels crushed, the one who lashes out, and the voice of authority—not malicious, but maintaining order by decree rather than dialogue. All agreed that in every story, the sequence of what happened was the same: things got progressively worse. We thought the most dramatic change was in the story in which the window was broken. We were fortunate to have a set designer who built us a beautiful brick corner wall with a nine-pane window featuring breakaway (sugar-based) glass. Our music director helped the cast refine and arrange their phrases into lyrics and then produced a dynamic melody. We wound up with a powerful three-voice song that dramatically captured the cast's take on what happens when people refuse to listen to one another.

Does It Have to Come to This?

Singer 1
Can't you hear my cry
That lingers deep inside
I try to have an equal voice
You push me to the side

Singer 3 (spoken)
I don't want to talk about it
I'm in control here
Think! You're just kids

Singer 2
Can't you feel my rage
We're not monsters in your cage
I will always stand my ground
You cannot keep me bound

Singer 3 (spoken)
I don't want to talk about it
I'm still the one in control here
Just listen to me

Singer 1
I can't take this anymore

I'm tired of being ignored
You no longer have a choice
Now you'll hear my voice

Singer 2
No! I won't stay in my place
I won't do an about-face

Singers 1 & 2
Stop! And listen to me
I will always stand for what I believe

Singer 3 (spoken)
Will you stop that
Sit down
I'm sick of this
Just listen to me, please!
I am still in control
Be quiet!
Just listen to me right now!

[During a musical bridge, Singers 1 and 2 try to get a response from Singer 3. She turns them away. Exasperated, they start to fight between themselves. Singer 3 pulls them apart. Singer 1 buries her face in her hands. Singer 2 goes to the window, picks up a brick, turns to give Singer 3 a nasty look, and then defiantly smashes the window with the brick.]

Singers 1 & 2
We will stop at nothing
We will take on any risk
Can't we work this out together
Or does it have to come to this?

Singer 3 (spoken softly)
Does it have to come to this?

Singer 1
Can't you hear my

Singers 1, 2, & 3 (in harmony)
Cry?

The title of the song was taken from the penultimate line: "Does it have to come to this?" The cast realized that this was something that united all the voices; no one wanted the situation to turn out this way. The cast decided that the final line, echoing the opening, "Can't you hear my cry?" should be sung in three-part harmony, so as to communicate a sense of how all three were desperately trying to be heard.

I appreciated these young actors' impulse to characterize the human side of the authority figure. As tempting as it is to create dramatic one-dimensional villains, the process of analyzing these stories encourages the actors to take a close look at why people behave the way they do, and that includes all the players in the event, not just the kids involved. Their task is to show how the different sides lock horns, not to show who was right or who should win. After unpacking their stories, they decided their authority figure was not intrinsically evil, just convinced the best way to avoid problems was to keep a lid on any kind of disruptive activity. Her behavior was at cross-purposes to the other two, who wanted to be heard and were blinded by distress and outrage when denied the opportunity.

There may be cases in which the cast feels it is important to make a piece about a singularly destructive or malicious way of behaving. But even then, the group can do better than to create a cartoon villain. You can encourage cast members to identify truthfully what it is that enables their bad guy to succeed. They can design a piece to show exactly how he operates, how he convinces people to support him, and what the consequences of his actions are. They can shine a light on where in this relationship lies the hope for positive change. They can reveal what they believe to be the source for healing. There's plenty of material there for theatre. Anyone can show a cardboard cutout, moustache-twirling scoundrel, but that won't promote understanding about the root of the problem or about what it takes to improve the situation.

Sample Two: A Physical Theatre Scene

On another occasion, five actors ranging in age from nine to seventeen unpacked stories about a time when "someone puts down your friend while you're standing there and you don't know what to do." One story took place on an elementary school playground during recess. Another took place in the prep line of a fast-food restaurant while working the afternoon shift. A third happened one Sunday going into church. The fourth had happened several years before while on a visit with relatives in another state. The fifth was read from a newspaper story. The circumstances of these five stories were as different as they could be, but they all had that one thing in common. The actors harvested a wide range of material from the different stories. There were a number of lyrical phrases, but a couple of astonishing analogous images led us toward developing a physical theatre scene rather than a song. (I'll say more on those images later.) As it turned out, the phrases unpacked from the stories tended—with a few exceptions—to reflect the thoughts of those involved rather than what they said aloud. The phrases were drawn from what the storytellers said as well as from other cast members' personal recollections of similar experiences. The actors did generate phrases associated with the person delivering the put-downs but, for this piece, we decided to focus only on the points of view of the one being targeted and the bystander:

Victim's Thoughts

I've got a right to be here.
Why are you bothering me?
I was just minding my own business and you had to bother me.
I didn't ask for this.
Leave me alone.
I know who I am.
I don't care what you think.
I'm in this all by myself again.

Bystander's Thoughts

They're just arguing—there's nothing I can do.
If I don't say anything, it's like saying it's okay.
I don't know what I should say . . .
I don't want to get him/her mad at me . . .
It won't amount to anything.
It's just going back and forth.
If they're not actually hurting each other, why get involved?
I might get hurt.
Is she okay?
What does she want me to do?
You can't say that!
You can't do that!
I'm just standing here, I don't know what's going on.
I won't do anything unless fighting starts.
[after it's over] I should have done something. I should've said something. I should've . . .

Striking Gestures

observer's eyes looking blank and surprised
people stuck, not moving while it's happening
people fumbling with what they're doing while it's happening
people turning their heads away

We described the rhythmic version of this kind of situation as a tick-tock, tick-tock, counterpoint percussion, or two-note string plucking that started quietly and steadily increased in intensity and volume.

While focusing on turning points, the actors clarified a progression of actions extrapolated from several stories and, again, drawn from their own experiences. The actions represented points along a continuum from the most subtle instance of a put-down to the most extreme:

1. giving someone a rude look/rolling your eyes
2. pointing
3. sticking out your tongue
4. whispering or saying something aside (to someone else)
5. making rude gestures/stomping

6. calling someone names to his or her face (from slight to harsh)
7. overpowering/physically dominating the person
8. hitting
9. fighting/hurting
10. torturing/killing

This was serious stuff. The cast tried to think up a comedy equivalent of a situation in which a person is attacked or abused while another stands by. Someone proposed a Three Stooges routine, with Moe clobbering Curly while Larry looks on. I solicited other ideas for preexisting material (rhymes, stories, pictures, or characters) that reflected the quality or spirit of the experience. Someone suggested, "Sticks and stones can break my bones, but words can never hurt me."

And finally, while investigating the tools a week earlier, two actors had come up with a powerful image using a pillow and a wooden board.* The first actor sat on the floor minding her own business, and the second tried to get a rise out of her by bopping her on the head with a pillow. Failing to get a response after several attempts, the second actor dropped the pillow, picked up the board, and reared back, ready to swing at the first actor's head. That was the end of their presentation. If she had simply picked up the board to begin with, we in the audience would have wondered, "What is she going to do?" But the fact that we had seen the action played out once already with the pillow allowed us to project very vividly in our minds what was now about to happen with much more serious consequences. Everyone in the group gasped. That image had stayed with us and, as we worked on this piece about an attack, we decided to include it in the list.

There were, of course, other images and elements put forward for this piece but these were the ones we selected. Here is how our piece took shape: We wanted to establish the subject right from the beginning. It would open with younger cast members brightly singing "Sticks and stones . . ." The song was familiar enough that it would give everyone in the audience a general idea of what the scene was going to address. Then, inspired by the Three Stooges comedy routine idea, and drawing upon the repeated-with-a-variation image of the pillow and board, the actors would play out the entire continuum of put-downs twice: once harmlessly and humorously as a comedy routine, and a second time straight, with absolute seriousness, up to and including a killing. In fact, a few years earlier in our city, a man had been clubbed to death with a bat in a racially motivated attack, a story about which the cast was fully aware. We identified a comedic equivalent for each step in the continuum (the specific stage business was actually worked out, with much hilarity, a few weeks later in rehearsal), including a party-razz to represent sticking out a tongue; maliciously aimed farts to represent verbal attacks; windup chatter teeth to represent fear; and a bonk on the head with

*Not every group of actors will be safety-conscious enough to work with potentially dangerous tools like a wooden board. This particular group had earned my trust.

an oversized, inflated plastic bat to represent physical violence. We added sound effects to highlight the comedy. The second time around, the scene would reveal realistically what the cast had observed about the way an exchange of this kind progresses. The phrases would be used directly as spoken text and the gestures would be incorporated.

The character doing the put-downs meticulously played out each of the stages of abuse. The first time through it was very funny when, at the climax, he pulled out the inflated plastic bat, bonked the other actor on the head, and birdies chirped. The bonked one staggered around while her friend stood by, bewildered, shrugging his shoulders and scratching his head. The second time through, the progression of parallel incidents stood out in marked contrast to the first. It ended with the abuser pulling out a realistic-looking bat and clubbing the victim to death while the friend stood by not knowing what to do.

The actors were very clear about including the most striking phrase they associated with the experience of awkwardly standing by after a friend has been put down. After a stunned silence, the friend repeatedly stuttered, "Oh, I should have . . . I should've . . . I should've. . . . To end the piece, the younger actors brightly and chillingly repeated their singsong verse: "Sticks and stones can break my bones, but words can never hurt me."

We discovered in rehearsal that, in the comedy section of the piece, it was too easy to feel sympathy for the actor getting pummeled. If the first half didn't work as comedy, the second half wouldn't work as drama. So we tried making it easier to laugh at the first half by depersonalizing the actors. They performed the comedy portion wearing commedia dell'arte–style character half-masks: two goofy-looking half-masks for the friends and one malevolent-looking mask for the bully. It helped. By obscuring the actors' faces and making them more clownlike or cartoonlike, we made it much easier for the audience to enjoy the physical comedy. The addition of masks also gave us a clue about how to make a clear transition to the second section. After the comedy victim recovered from having been bonked on the head, the abuser pulled out a (fake) knife and, with one motion, cut the strap of the other actor's mask. It fell away, revealing her human face. Her companion/bystander lifted his own mask to his forehead in astonishment, revealing his human face. To keep the attention on them, the abuser remained masked. The realism of the second half now played in stark contrast to the first half. Also, because the phrases were conceived of as inner thoughts, we found many of them didn't seem to fit when spoken aloud. We decided the actors would pantomime their exchange, using the gestures identified beforehand and adding more as needed for clarity. Other actors on a platform well above the stage floor would say the lines.

This was an atypical scene for a show with kids. It included ten cast members of different races and ages, four singing "Sticks and Stones," three playing out the interaction, and three providing comedy sound effects and then voicing the inner thoughts of the two principal characters. The actors made use of masks, props, sounds, gestures, text, and song. We also used music: a prerecorded carnival-like soundtrack during the first section, which was abruptly silenced the instant the first mask came off. The scene did not include traditional dialogue, an identifiable setting, or a realistic situation. And yet, what sounds a little abstract when described on paper was electrifying in the theatre. It is an example of the way a scene does not have to rely on literal narrative and realistic dialogue to make a valuable and powerful point about human behavior. Sample five will illustrate the creation of a scene that incorporates more realistic dialogue.

Sample Three: Choreography

A group of actors investigating tools crafted an image that dramatically evoked the hurt of exclusion. Using a six-foot-long, half-inch diameter, flexible plastic PVC pipe, one actor was able to form a hoop by grasping each end of the pipe and bending it. She could enclose three girls in her "circle of friends" and exclude a fifth girl. All at once, three of the four decided one girl in the circle was no longer welcome. With one deft move, the actor holding the hoop flipped it up, swung it around, and left the evicted one standing outside of it. There was clearly enormous potential here for transforming the social dynamics of inclusion and exclusion into something concrete. We regrouped and unpacked stories about aspects of that kind of experience: the allure of belonging to a group, hierarchies within a group, the tenuous nature of membership, the desperation of potential rejection, and the impact of expulsion. These actors were becoming adept at thinking in visual terms and they now worked to translate or explain these social dynamics using the hoop. The moves were refined and organized. The final choreography, involving more dancers and more hoops, was worked out in rehearsal. In this piece, dance was used to tangibly illuminate patterns and subtle variations in social behavior.

Another layer of this piece, which for lack of time was never fully developed, involved the sound of laughter. During the unpacking process, we identified laughter as a sound associated with rejection from a group *as well as* a sound associated with belonging to a group. When something pops up in more than one place on an Unpacking List, it should be seen as a little flag saying "There's something worth exploring here!" It signals potential for revealing an experience from different angles. The sound of laughter would have added another dimension to the piece. The actors could have spent some time characterizing many different kinds of laughter and authentically capturing the quality of each. They could have used their voices to show the ways in which laughter is used to include and exclude, underscoring the dancers' movements with parallels in sound.

Sample Four: A Spoken Chorus

While developing a show dealing with kids' own perceptions about the things that influence the directions of their lives, the cast told stories about experiences they felt had changed them. The stories were unexpectedly consistent. Every one of twenty cast members described a time in which he or she first experienced independence. From the eight-year-old who felt pride at first putting her own coin in the city bus fare slot, to the adolescent whose parents let him and his brother explore the fairgrounds by themselves, to the teenager who got herself into recovery and freed herself of alcohol abuse, achieving something on their own had been a major turning point in their lives. We developed an extensive list of those moments and, by considering the opposite, we developed a contrasting list of what had come before. They identified earlier, parallel moments in which dependence on their families, teachers, and so on had helped them feel secure.

Looking over the list, we decided it was clearly destined to be a text-based piece, but as lyrical as the phrases were, the sheer number of them seemed far too complicated to turn into a song. It needed a unifying element, something to help the phrases fit together. Since the piece was to be about the actual moment of undergoing change, we considered what would convey a sense of immediacy. I remembered a three-word refrain from a script I'd read years before and suggested we try using it here to see if it served our purposes.[11] We put the most significant words of each account into present tense and preceded each one with the phrase "Now I am . . ." We then peppered the mix with lines such as "I can do it" and "I am able to," so as to reflect the actors' self-descriptions of having achieved this sense of independence. To help tie the piece together, we picked one story, about a lost young girl's brave trek alone through the streets of Manhattan, and spread it through the course of the text. Her very concrete achievement, finally making it back home by herself, served handily to close the piece.

The poet W. H. Auden once described the process of writing and revising a poem as being similar to the process of trying to call to mind an old telephone number. You've got the numbers in your head, or most of them, so you try saying them aloud in different orders until it sounds right. We followed his lead and fiddled with the order of our phrases until the bounce and rhythm sounded right. It needed no elaborate staging. Twelve actors stood choir-style and simply spoke the words, occasionally speaking in unison to create texture. This is how the text looked in the script:

Independence

Nora & Skye: Now I am with my parents

Jonah & Rebecca: Now I am with my mom

Lynzee: Now I am with my dad

Skye & Nora: Now I am with my sister

Rebecca, Jonah, & Lynzee: Now I am with my brother

Nora: Now we are taking the bus

Juan: Now we are getting on the bus

Nora & Skye: Now mom pays the driver

Jonah: Now mom tells me when to ring the bell

Carlotta & Lynzee: Now we are getting off the bus

Sasha, Nora, Juan, Rebecca, & Skye: Now I am with my parents

Nora: Now I am waiting by myself

Jonah: Now I have my own bus ticket in my hand

Nora: Now my mom is at home

Carlotta: Now I'm on the bus

Skye: Now I'm being allowed

Rebecca: Now I'm allowing myself

Skye: Now I'm independent

Nora: Now I know I can

Skye & Nora: Now I

Sasha, Juan, & Rebecca: I can

Jonah: I am able to

Nora: I can

Rebecca: Now I am with my family driving in a van

Beckie: Squeezed into a little seat

Carlotta: Squeezed for days

Rebecca: A little seat driving along for days

Beckie, Rebecca, & Carlotta: With my family

Matsya: Now I am traveling with my family

Jason: Now I am traveling with my family

Nora, Matsya, Juan, & Jason: Brothers

Jonah, Rebecca, & Sasha: Sisters

Sasha & Skye: Traveling with my family

Jason: Now I'm by myself

Kali: Eugene

Jason: Macon, Georgia

Lynzee: One Hundred and Eighth Street in New York City

Kali: Now I gotta get home

Lynzee: Now I gotta get back

Kali: I'm by myself

Rebecca: Help!

Kali: Now I'm figuring it out

Jason: Now I'm handling it

Matsya: Now I'm finding a way home

Lynzee: Now I'm figuring it out

Beckie: Now I'm looking at a map

Rebecca: Now I'm remembering

Matsya: Now I'm handling it

Lynzee: Now I'm walking. Ninety-Sixth Street

Jason: Strangers

Matsya: Friends

Lynzee: Scared

Carlotta: Fun

Juan: By myself

Jason: Now I'm halfway there

Sasha: Now I've found a place to stay

Lynzee: Now I'm walking. Seventy-Eighth Street

Nora, Kali, Rebecca, Matsya, & Juan: Now I'm doing it

Jason, Juan, Sasha, & Carlotta: Now I am allowing myself to

Skye & Jonah: Now I know I can
Juan: Now I'm being taken to the county fair
Carlotta: Now I'm being taken to Disneyland!
Nora: Now I'm being taken to the bakery
Sasha: Now I'm being taken skiing
Jonah: Here's money
Beckie: Have fun
Kali: See you later
Juan: See you later
Jason: Meet here later
Kali: Have fun
Juan: My brother and me
Jonah: By ourselves
Juan: Just us
Matsya, Kali, & Beckie: Allowed
Juan: We can do it
Jonah: Now we can
Rebecca, Sasha, & Jason: They know we can
Lynzee: Fifty-First Street
Sasha: Now I'm making it work
Kali: Now I'm organizing the whole thing
Juan: Now it's a success
Skye: Now I'm making a difference to other people
Jason: Now I'm working on myself
Kali: Now I'm getting clean and sober
Matsya: Now I'm putting it all together
Juan: They trust me
Beckie: They know I can do it
Kali: I know
Lynzee: Thirty-Seventh Street
Beckie: Now I flattened him
Matsya: Now I found out he's a ninth grader!
Sasha: Now I'm on the ski lift by myself

Carlotta: Now I'm at the audition by myself
Skye: Now I'm teaching myself how
Jason: Now I'm setting myself up with an agent in Hollywood
Juan: Now I'm on the East Burnside bus and I'm okay
Skye: Now I'm watching out for my brother and sister
Beckie: Now I'm watching out for myself
Rebecca, Matsya, & Jonah: Now I can do it
Nora, Kali, & Juan: I can
Kali: I am able to
Jonah: I'm figuring it out
Carlotta, Sasha, & Jason: I'm handling it
Skye & Matsya: I'm finding a way
Beckie: Now I'm figuring it out
Rebecca: Now I made it
Lynzee: Eighteenth Street
Kali: Seven years old
Lynzee: I made it

In this piece, the initial question, "What has really changed you?" revealed something about which the actors hadn't ever given much thought. The process of building the piece helped them recognize how significant the act of exerting their own independence had been for them. When they performed it, the reaction from the audience was tremendous. Many adults reported how the piece had revived in them deep feelings about their own transformative experiences of moving toward independence. They had been reminded of the importance of having an opportunity to find one's own way. Some parents confided that, despite fears for their children venturing out in these dangerous times, they were going to think twice about being overly protective in the future.

Sample Five: A Dialogue Scene

Let's say a cast has decided to create a piece based on a Topic Card that simply reads, "diversity—the good things about being different." The actors tell stories about some things in their experiences that reflect that idea. Someone describes a time when a group project in class was successful because of all the different ideas contributed by the diverse participants. During the unpacking, the cast determines the project itself was in the category of all those things that are only successful when diverse. What else is in that category? They list a patchwork quilt, which by definition is successful only when diverse; a rain forest, as compared to an apple orchard; and a symphony orchestra, as compared to one hundred identical instruments.

They propose that the opposite of the cooperation described in that story would be a situation in which someone insists that his way is the only way to solve a problem. Some of the actors have experienced individuals who try to foist their plans and their plans alone on a supposedly cooperative group. Those actors generate a list of the phrases associated with that situation. They aim to be scrupulously honest so as not to make a parody, but to authentically capture the essence of the exchange. How does this person interrupt the proceedings? What are the actual things she says when she claims that there's just one way of solving a problem? The group members work out the text of the interrupter, drawing on what they've experienced. They identify the phrases they've heard people use to disparage diversity of opinion and they identify the phrases they've heard used to counter that point of view:

> Well, that's a stupid idea!
> I'm sorry! I can't do it that way!
> I've done this kind of thing before and it never works . . .
> We're running out of time.
> Let's just try it once and see what happens.

They also list the gestures (the waving of hands, a look expressing ridicule), and the sounds (the buzz of brainstorming activity, the scream of exasperation) or the lack of sounds (the silence of a group stuck by demoralization) associated with the experience.

They continue to unpack the story. They try to find the rhythmic or musical version of the experience. Someone picks up on the orchestra idea and suggests a musical version of diverse collaboration. She imagines having several different voices singing in harmony or a variety of instruments joining to make a musical whole that is richer than the sum of many identical voices singing in unison or identical instruments all playing the same notes.

They come to the exaggerated or comedy version. Everybody thinks of this at once—a person who tries to stop an orchestra because the musicians are "ruining" the music with all their different instruments and voices.

The cast and director step back to review what they've collected and suddenly the piece is born! The basic shape of the piece, inspired by the image of the musical version, will involve a group of singing voices. Perhaps one begins alone and another joins to make a harmony, then a third joins, then a fourth adds the sound of an instrument, and so on. Right in the middle of the music, someone from the group calls the whole thing to a crashing halt. They are all ruining the music! He has a better plan. The characters start hashing it out. Not only have the cast members identified the key elements of the dialogue they will insert here, they also have on hand all sorts of gestures, sounds, and silences that define the exchange. All are brought in at this point. The actors know how the exchange starts and how it progresses. They extrapolate the intent of a single phrase to a few lines. They fit in the response, maybe as text, maybe as gesture, maybe as sound. They expand upon another phrase and fit it in. Before long, the group has developed a textured, realistic scene that is far more complex than just the words of dialogue.

Where does it go from here? That depends on what the cast members have found in comparing their stories. What have they determined about the nature of situations like these? How do these situations get resolved? Based on their experiences, does an interrupter generally succeed in convincing others to follow his plan? What happens next? Perhaps he does, and they all start singing his song in unison. Perhaps one voice irreverently slips into harmony and before long the whole group is off on a full-voice harmonic collaboration again. Perhaps the cast members have noticed a pattern that's helped them figure out what gets an interrupter to see things in a different way. They translate what they've found into physical or musical terms and resolve the piece that way. They continually review by asking themselves, "Is this how it happens? Is this accurate? Have we captured the truth of it? What's missing?" And then they revise.

If the group gets stuck, a helpful step is to review the turning points. Focus on showing how the event happens: what happens first, what happens next. The cast can always generate more text by asking: What are the words and phrases that are in the air before this moment happens? What are the words you hear at each turning point? What are the last things you hear as it is ending?

What originated as stories about good experiences with diverse groups has become a piece of theatre that metaphorically reveals what makes diversity interesting and exciting. It illustrates kids' perceptions about ways in which efforts to work collaboratively are undermined. The presentation of voices singing in harmony makes the piece much more fun to watch and listen to than a simple reenactment of one of the initial stories, yet it draws realistic elements from the experiences of many cast members. It has a beginning, a middle, and an end. It's funny. And best of all, the performance will be passionate and vigorous because each member of the cast is fully aware of what the group is trying to get across and why. It's their material.

Sample Six: Monologues

In the previous example, a cast was able to start with emblematic phrases and expand them into text for dialogue. The same can certainly be done to create a monologue. A range of stories all inspired by one Topic Card may yield a very consistent way of thinking; phrases from different Unpacking Lists may turn out to represent various shades of a single point of view. Conversely, the phrases may wind up reflecting two or more conflicting ways of seeing a problem. In either case, the phrases can serve as key points in a monologue. It may take the shape of a soliloquy, in which a character weighs the different aspects of a problem aloud. This is the classic form of monologue, the most famous (in English) being "To be or not to be. . . ." from *Hamlet*. Or they may choose to create a testimonial-style monologue, that is, a monologue in which a character tells a story.

The actors begin by sorting the material into an organized progression. They identify which of the phrases, gestures, and so on capture the sense of where this person's thinking starts, which ones capture the sense of where it moves from there, and which ones capture the sense of a resolution. They expand on the intent of each phrase and fill in around the edges with more words until it works as speech. For a soliloquy-style monologue, they can concentrate on simply articulating what the problem is, where the conflicts lie, and what's at stake. The specific identity of the speaker may actually be decided upon later, when the time comes to figure out how the show fits together. For a testimonial-style monologue, the actors can look at the resolution signified by the final phrases. They can consider what situations would lead a person to come to that conclusion. Working backward, they can invent a scenario, some event or relationship that led this character to feel the way he does, fitting the progression of phrases and gestures into the monologue.

Sample Seven: Rearranging Existing Texts

An audience's familiarity with well-known characters and situations can offer a real advantage for communicating meaning. The cast can play with expectations and twist traditions to create emphasis. Let's say a group of actors is working on a piece about the ways people successfully offer support and help to one another. They've made a list of the kinds of people who help others, including comic book superheroes. Consider the opportunities for comedy *and* drama when they thrust a helpful superhero into the ward of an AIDS hospice. Here he is—in full costume, complete with foam rubber pecs under his suit—a problem solver accustomed to saving the day. But his bulky muscles and x-ray vision are of no use to him here. He can't reverse a terminal illness with super powers. The cast designs his scene such that he has to figure out what he *can* do. The dialogue, the gestures, and so on reflect what they know. For anyone in the audience who has felt powerless in the face of having a loved one slowly die, this costumed superhero serves as metaphor and guide.

Or suppose the cast is working on a piece about making difficult decisions. In the course of unpacking and comparing stories, they've clarified some of the social dynamics that complicate the decision-making process. While considering opposites or while looking over analogous existing material, they have identified a couple of well-known fictional or historical characters. One makes decisions easily and authoritatively, perhaps Nancy Drew; the other is unsure about what she should do, perhaps Alice from *Alice's Adventures in Wonderland*. Cast members can bring in copies of the stories or historical accounts in which these characters appear. There they'll find source material for dialogue, character, and circumstance. They can dramatize the story with some adjustments. They can place the character known for her ability to make decisions into a situation where she must face the challenging social dynamics they've identified: Nancy Drew in a modern high school. What does confident Nancy do when she is continually tormented by other kids for being a "brain" or a "schoolgirl?" Or perhaps they can put her in the circumstances of the other character: Nancy Drew in Wonderland. The ways in which a teenage girl can use her intelligence to deal with a tough situation will become very evident when Nancy is up against the Queen of Hearts or the Hatter. To develop the text and staging for their piece, the cast can make use of phrases and situations associated with this character as well as all the elements they've generated, their own emblematic phrases, gestures, sounds, and so on. The audience will recognize how the character traditionally behaves, and this new situation can be used to clarify the forces she's now up against. The piece can highlight the social dynamics that cause even a self-assured character to have difficulty making decisions.

Sample Eight: Incorporating Existing Texts

Instead of rearranging something familiar, the cast may choose to rely on the existing relationships in a well-known story or a set of characters to create emphasis. For example, in a piece about facing a challenge, the cast might have found an interesting parallel in the old story of "The Three Billy Goats Gruff." In Asbjørsen's tale, a young goat wants to get to the green pasture on the other side of a bridge, but he's stopped by the threatening troll who lives under it. The goat fetches his bigger brother to deal with the troll. Bigger brother is intimidated and gets the biggest brother. Ultimately after biggest brother dispatches the troll, all the goats enjoy the green grass on the other side of the bridge. Why not use it? The events dramatically illustrate some important aspects of the issue. As he approaches his obstacle, the little billy goat deals with procrastination, deferring responsibility to someone else, and a fear of the challenge. Perfectly realistic lines about getting started could be humorously layered with the trip-trap sounds of crossing the bridge. The actors could have fun mixing the troll's lines about poking out eyeballs and crushing body and bones to bits with their own realistic lines about anxiety over dealing with the problem. The events provide the actors with a structure on which to hang what would otherwise be fragmentary material.[12]

Sample Nine: Staging Existing Texts

It may be that the cast members work and work on an idea, defining the specific nature of a situation, discovering patterns and subtle nuances, gathering phrases and gestures, and then while brainstorming and researching analogous material, they come upon an existing story that already says everything they want to say in their piece. By all means, use the story as is. The actors have become like the repairman in the old joke who gets paid an enormous fee for fixing the fabulously complicated machine. He walks in to the room, pulls out a small hammer and taps a flange. Voila! The machine is fixed. When the boss complains that the repairman sure gets a lot of money for just one simple tap with a hammer, the fellow replies, "Ahhh . . . but it's knowing *where* to tap!" Out of all the thousands upon thousands of stories in the world, the actors' work has led them to know just the right story to convey what they have in mind. Adapt it. Stage it. Let its appropriateness help them communicate their meaning.

On one occasion, I was working with some actors to create a piece about how individual young people can really make a difference in the world. Juan Williams had recently given a lecture I'd attended in which he spoke on this very subject. He is a journalist and the author of *Eyes on the Prize*, the companion book to PBS' television series about America's Civil Rights era. Williams related the story of Barbara Johns, a sixteen-year-old girl who attended a segregated school in the South during the early 1950s. Her ingenuity, her passionate belief in her cause, and her spirited determination led her to play an important role in *Brown v. Board of Education*, the landmark U.S. Supreme Court case that tore apart segregation in public schools.

Barbara Johns' story was a perfect illustration of what we were trying to convey. I located a transcript of that portion of his talk and proposed it to the cast as a possible monologue. The cast agreed the story was a good fit; I called Williams to ask permission to include it in our show, which he kindly granted.

In most cases, I encourage the cast members to do their own research, ask the questions, and find the material themselves. But this is a collaborative process and there is certainly no reason why a director cannot also bring in material to help solve the stage problems the group has put forward. The director can say, "I'd like to propose this as a way to solve the problem," or, "Yesterday I heard this in the discussion; let's focus on it."

Permissions

When making use of existing texts, keep in mind that someone may own the copyright to the material. There is a great deal of older material in the public domain that is free for use without question. More current material may be copyrighted, so you should contact the owner and ask for permission to use it. It is important to be conscientious, not only for legal reasons but for cultural reasons as well. Different cultures hold very different attitudes about the use and place of stories. A story that seems "really cool" to actors making a play may be part of the sacred cultural traditions of the group from which it originates. It also may be that the version of the story you've come across is a corruption of a more authentic version. Seek out those who can tell you more about the story and whether your group can be granted permission to use it.

You should encourage the actors to draw from their own cultural heritage but, as the group tries out ideas, it's always wise to treat cultural art forms with care and honor, not as decoration. Director/actress Rebecca Rice has noted that "ceremonies, rituals, services, and storytellings are not always meant to be observed, but experienced . . . the theatricalization of [some communities'] customs can amount to sacrilege." She relates her own experience of having tried to stage a gospel service. The presentation in a theatre before a passive audience led to an atmosphere that was campish, rather than holy.[13]

A basic rule of thumb is don't make any assumptions. Between a library, a phone book, and the Internet, you'll surely be able to contact those who can tell you more about that perfect story you've found.

More Suggestions

Incorporating the Tools

From the beginning of the script development workshop sessions, the actors have used the tools to explain to one another various aspects of their topic. As they construct the pieces, they should be encouraged to freely incorporate these objects into their staging. Rather than fill out a production with realistic props, the actors can use found objects, fabrics, and musical instruments to evoke the essence of the props they need.

Young actors can capitalize on society's traditional image of children pretending that ordinary objects are a variety of specific fixtures in their play world. But the truth is the technique is used far and wide by accomplished professional theatre artists. In his one-man show *Don't Start Me to Talking or I'll Tell Everything I Know . . .* , actor John O'Neal creates a multitude of environments with only a handful of objects. A tall stepladder becomes a convincing jail cell when he's standing beneath it. Later, he carefully opens the stepladder's hinged paint bucket shelf, now a bus station locker door, and peers inside with anticipation. A handkerchief used to wipe a brow later becomes a shoe shine rag, a book, and then a cup of coffee. It is particularly captivating because he doesn't call attention to the transformation of these objects. There is no magic or joke or punch line involved; he simply treats an object first as one thing and then as the next.

Using a few objects to evoke the essence of different items is a marvelous way to engage the audience in the fun of imaginative participation. As the audience members fill in the stage picture with their imaginations, they meet the actors halfway and share a part in creating those moments on stage.

Developing Full Characters

As the actors unpack the stories, they will come across behaviors and ways of perceiving situations that fly in the face of one another. When the actors are developing their characters, whether in scenes with dialogue, monologues, or songs, always encourage them to embrace the contradictions they find. Historian John Fuegi believes that the "conscious use of contradiction" is an essential element in all of Brecht's work. Fuegi writes:

> If, in one rehearsal, you have built up so-called "good qualities" in [a character], then be sure to bring out her so-called "negative" qualities in other rehearsals . . . And, as you do this, do not, repeat, do not, resolve the contradictions inherent in the method. Remember always that complex individuals and complex action are made up of multiple layers of contradictions. To reduce those contradictions is to have your characters become cardboard cutouts. The characters themselves may very well not be aware of the contradictions but the director needs to bring them out . . . . I would suggest that there is virtually no character in Brecht (with the exception of a very few out-and-out villains) who are not simultaneously at least two rather different characters. It is this simultaneous difference, these consciously unresolved contradictions that give these characters their depth.[14]

Incorporating our all-too-human contradictions also encourages the audience to take a second look at the circumstances. It encourages them to ask themselves what causes this character to do what she wouldn't ordinarily do.[15]

Bisociation

Arthur Koestler's extraordinary book *The Act of Creation* explores (among many things) that moment of truth common to science, art, and comedy in which human beings experience a cognitive leap. He coined the term *bisociation* to denote the perception of a situation or idea "in two self-consistent, but habitually incompatible frames of reference."[16] It describes the "A-ha!" that comes when one suddenly makes the connection or sees the joke. It is the moment of understanding when it dawns on a person that what he is seeing belongs to more than one category and that it has been a member of that second category all along. At that instant, the scientist makes a revolutionary breakthrough, suddenly grasping the significance of what's been right there in front of her. The artist surprises us by elegantly showing how one thing is related to another. And the comedian makes us laugh with a play on words or a visual pun in which what we think is one thing turns out to be something else. Koestler provides an intriguing analysis of this link between comic comparison, objective analogy, and poetic image. He argues that the logical pattern of all three is very much the same. And the point of understanding is the point at which revelation, astonishment, and delight all meet.

The mechanics of bisociation can be utilized to help make an illuminating and tremendously effective piece. In the course of unpacking stories, the actors identify one parallel after another. They will find many occasions in which images from two different ways of seeing will overlap. The cast can choose to layer a piece with visual or aural clues that tacitly imply a certain meaning, feeding the traditional assumptions. At the climax of the piece, they can reveal information that makes it clear that those clues also belong to another category. At that moment, the members of the audience confront their own assumptions about the second category.

A recent television public service announcement by the Urban Alliance on Race Relations made quite an impact in this way. The left half of the screen showed the face of Black man in his twenties with a shaved head. He looked straight at the camera. The right half of the screen punched up a long sentence, one or two words at a time, each line accompanied by a drumbeat:

> Michael Conrad,
> Male, Age 28,
> Armed Robbery,
> Assault and Battery,
> Rape,
> Murder,
> Apprehended
> January 1994 by
> Police Lieutenant
> Joseph Cruthers,
> shown here

How many viewers of all races were drawn into making almost unconscious judgments based on assumptions about what they were seeing, recognizing the fact that they'd done so only when the last line appeared?

One of the most discussion-provoking pieces I've ever directed was conceived of and performed by an Asian American teenager. In a fictional monologue written to take advantage of the concept of bisociation, the character described how she had been going out with Chris for almost a year. She talked about their relationship, particularly the difficulties they had due to other people's attitudes toward them as a couple. The speech and her performance made quite a case for the importance of tolerance. Their love for each other was strong enough to overcome the problems they faced with their nontraditional relationship. Many who saw the piece performed have described to me the automatic assumptions they made about Chris. In their minds, they sided with this young woman's character, thinking, "Why shouldn't she be able to go out with him, no matter what the difference in their culture or color of their skin?" It was only at the end of the monologue that the speaker used a pronoun for the first time and the audience realized Chris was also female.

Neither the Urban Alliance public service announcement nor the *Chris* speech deceives the audience. In retrospect, the man looks like a police officer; in retrospect, the speech is about a same-sex relationship; but both play on the audience's preconceptions in order to make an impact. What makes the use of this device particularly exciting is that the spectators become integrally involved. They take in information and make internal judgments based on their preconceived opinions of this situation. Had they been given the opportunity to compare—"Do you see how A is like B?"—many of them would dismiss the comparison as irrelevant or come up with all sorts of logical arguments about why the two are not the same at all. But now they have committed themselves in their minds. The artists have allowed the spectators to confirm their assumptions.

Then, suddenly, it becomes apparent that this story is about something else altogether. The facts, though, have remained the same. Members of the audience find themselves calling into question their own preconceptions about this alternate meaning. Are their preconceptions valid after all? The use of bisociation in this context allows for an audience participation in which people become involved in the play via their imaginations and sociocultural expectations. Once they figuratively lure audience members up on stage, the actors take them through a transformational experience.

Fun

Here is one final thought about creating these performance pieces: whether they are serious or comic, don't forget to make the performances fun for the audience. So often our plays about social issues are terribly solemn. We hammer our points, thud, thud, thud, onto the heads of the audience. People don't come to the theatre to be bludgeoned! There is tremendous potential in this work to create a thrilling experience for the audience. Try to make your theatre with the aim of encouraging the audience members to watch the course of the action with all the enthusiasm that they might watch a sporting event, full of glee one moment and outrage the next. Design the performance with the idea that, as with a sporting event, the spectators should come away from it full of opinions about what they have seen: "It didn't have to be that way!" "She should've done this!" "He could've done that!" "If he'd only . . ." "Well, he was up against . . ." "Did you see that one time, the way she dealt with the . . ." "You know what I would've done if it were me. . . ."

Brecht passionately believed that one does not have to choose between a theatre that educates and one that entertains. He felt it was a false dichotomy. And he wasn't talking about simply adding a sugar coating to make the medicine go down, a few jokes mixed in with the message. He believed that the very processes of human social behavior, some familiar, some unexpected, could be at once revelatory and a great source of delight and enjoyment. It was the stuff of vital theatre. See if your group can prove him right.

4 WEAVING INDIVIDUAL PERFORMANCE PIECES INTO A SHOW

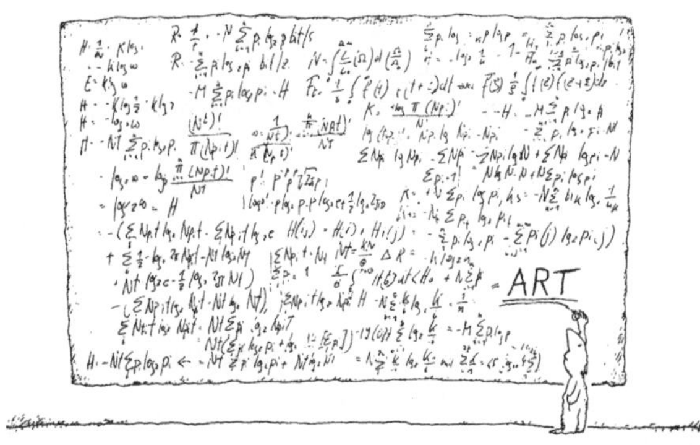

Magi Wechsler

For those planning to create an entire show, the time comes to finish up work on individual pieces, take stock of what you've got, and find some way to put it all together. It may seem a little daunting but, if you need reassurance, consider the story of Betty Comden and Adolph Green. Comden and Green were a New York–based writing team assigned in 1950 to develop an original script for a Metro-Goldwyn-Mayer film. They were accustomed to writing their own material from beginning to end, but this project was different. They were told to rummage through a stack of somebody else's songs, decide which ones they liked, and patch together a dozen or so into a movie. After a little grumbling, they picked through the sheet music, invented a throughline, and put together a script that went on to become one of the best-loved musicals in American film history: *Singin' in the Rain*, with Gene Kelly, Donald O'Connor, and Debbie Reynolds. And that film actually has a story line. Your group may ultimately find ways to put together material using an entirely nontraditional, non-narrative format.[17]

If you and your cast have done your work well, you've now produced quite a stack of papers. There are drafts of monologues, scenes with sections of dialogue and stage directions. There may be song lyrics with rudimentary compositions or with notes about ideas for melodies, rhythms, or styles written in the margins. There may be outlines for choreography and descriptions, drawings, or photocopies of stage pictures that will somehow be reflected in the show.

MAKING ABBREVIATED DESCRIPTIONS

A good first step toward finding a successful unifying structure is to look over the pieces you've all created so far. To help facilitate a collaborative effort, the group can write abbreviated descriptions of each piece on separate cards or pieces of paper. For example, the cards might read: "the duet about finding out you're pregnant," "the silk fabric scene about the polluted river," or "the build-up-to-a-fight choreography." It is now easier to organize and reorganize the pieces by simply moving the cards around on a bulletin board or table.

There are no hard and fast rules for any of this work, certainly none for weaving the pieces together. Ultimately, the show's topic is the unifying element; all the pieces relate to it in one way or another. The challenge now is to find a structure that will organize the pieces and put them into a logical progression that moves the show along from beginning to end. Let's consider some potential structures, keeping in mind that these are only a few possibilities.

Narrative

One way to tie together a script is to integrate the pieces into a familiar or invented story. By now the actors are increasingly able to characterize a story according to what the characters *do* instead of just describing the events in the plot. They may say that *The Wizard of Oz* is about someone who is taken away from her home, from everything familiar, and who tries to get back home. They will be able to identify parallels between what Dorothy does and something in their own experience.

The events of a well-known tale, its beginning, middle, and end, may provide just the framework your cast members need to unify all of their separate pieces. I have shown how the cast can create a single performance piece by adapting well-known source material. The actors work their own phrases, gestures, and sounds into the structure of a story that already exists. It may be that one of the stories or characters they have come upon lends itself to a broader application. If the cast has found a story that truly exhibits insightful and humorous parallels to the social dynamics of the topic they are exploring, they can similarly integrate all their scenes, songs, monologues, and so forth into that one story.

Alternatively, they may have developed one or more particularly strong characters or scenes and want to expand those scenes and characters to create an original story. One scene or song may stand out as the clearest representation of what the cast hopes to communicate. It can form the heart of the show, with the other pieces leading up to it or following it. The cast members may be so pleased with one or more of the characters that they want to devise a story to fit around them, an original narrative the characters can inhabit.

The Main Task and What Happens Along the Way

If the group decides to adapt or invent a narrative-based story to use as a unifying structure, a good first step is to consider two things: What is the main task in the story? and What happens along the way? The task is the throughline; it provides the structure. In *The Wizard of Oz*, Dorothy's task is to get back to Kansas. After the twister takes her to Oz, all the events in the story happen either as interruptions, diversions, or results of her attempt to get home. Cinderella wants to escape her miserable situation, even briefly, to go to the ball. Enter the Fairy Godmother. From that moment on, wheels are put in motion. Her task—to escape—dictates all that follows.

What happens along the way as the protagonist tries to fulfill the task are the places in which the various pieces can be fit. For example, on her journey to fulfill her task, a character meets someone who tells her a story. It is one of the monologues developed by the cast. Later in the story, there is a confrontation with some other characters. It leads her to sing a song, or perhaps others sing a song, underscoring the situation she's in. One by one, the scenes in the story—what happens along the way—are all slightly adjusted to fit into the narrative.

A Series of Episodes

The alternative to fitting the pieces into a story is to use a non-narrative-based structure. In traditional narrative theatre, the purpose of the scenes is to progressively unfold the plot. You may, however, choose simply to string the pieces together and let what happens within each scene contribute to a cumulative understanding of the play's meaning. The play becomes a vehicle to present episodes. Individual segments can be separated by blackouts, musical segues, or some other device. Although titles identifying each segment can be displayed on stage, announced by a narrator, or listed along with explanatory information in the program, they may not be necessary.

Place

One nonnarrative structure that can unify disparate pieces is setting. In 1986, Jim Cartwright wrote a haunting play about the desperate lives of a handful of poverty-stricken people in the British underclass. The play features a series of episodes about a range of men and women, all different ages, each responding to his or her circumstances in different ways. The unifying element? They all live on the same road. *Road* is not only the title of the play, it is the peg on which Cartwright hung all these lives. This is how the play opens:

> *Blackness. A match is struck. It is held underneath a broken road sign. The name part has been ripped off . . . only the word "Road" is left. The sign is very old and has been this way a long time.*
>
> Scullery: It's been broken.

The flame moves across to illuminate a man's face. He holds the match there until it goes out; at the same time a spotlight creeps up on his face.

Scullery: Wid' your night yous chose to come and see us. Wid' our night as usual we's all getting ready and turning out for a drink. THIS IS OUR ROAD! But tonight it's your Road an' all! Don't feel awkward wi' us, make yoursels at home. You'll meet 'all-sorts' down here I'm telling you love, an owt can happen tonight; he might get a bird, she might ha' a fight, she might. Let's shove off downt' Road and find out! We'll go house by house. Come on. Watch the kerb, missus. Here we go! Road's coming round us. (*He starts laughing, laughing uproariously.*)

Blackout.[18]

Some scripts rely on a narrator to guide the audience and interpret the events. The narrator holds everything together with all the authority of a master of ceremonies; if he were to leave, the audience would be lost and the show would collapse. In *Road*, Scullery has a much more modest contribution. He introduces the audience to the world of the play but then the life of the road pretty much takes over. It's the road that gives cohesion to the play. That one unifying element allows the playwright extraordinary freedom to show all kinds of experiences, including nondialogue, gesture-based scenes, without any obvious plot or narrative throughline. Although stories and plots of a sort unfold within each episode, there is no grand narrative climax. The show concludes with Scullery announcing that daybreak is coming soon. There are tableaux of the various characters engaged in what they do in the wee hours of the morning. Scullery says: "If you're ever in the area call again. Call again." And it's over. The place itself has provided a throughline, an environment where all sorts of related experiences can exist side by side.

A Prop

The 1993 film *Twenty Bucks* is about people's relationship to money. Two dozen episodes are all beautifully strung together, following a single twenty dollar bill from one person to the next as it is spent, given away, or found over the course of several days. There is a nod toward plot as a few characters show up more than once but, in general, the segments work independently. The simple presence of that prop in each segment unifies the whole film. Its movement from person to person is all that is needed to propel the action and provide perfectly acceptable transitions.

A Single Image or Metaphor

At the outset of a show, a single defining image or metaphor can help establish what unifies everything to follow. An exemplary image or metaphor may be found within one of the pieces the cast has already developed, or it may be formulated after reviewing all the pieces together. In a show I worked on about how people treat one another across lines of difference or perceived difference, the pieces we created fell into two categories. Some focused on what it is about diversity that tears people apart, and some focused on what it is about diversity that brings people together. We put all of the former into the first act, the latter into the second act. We established the contrast, and the structure, by creating a prologue incorporating the Chinese ideogram *Wei Chi*, which translates as *crisis*. Each performance began with an actor who came on stage and painted the Chinese characters in large strokes on a wall at the center of the set. She spoke to the audience about living in a time of crisis, and explained that, in Chinese, the character that means *crisis* is made up of two parts. The first part, *Wei*, is *danger*. She struck a match and held up the flame. The second part, *Chi*, is *opportunity*. She brought the flame down and used it to light a small candle. The large painted image remained there prominently throughout the show, reinforcing the division printed in the audience's program: Act I—Danger, Act II—Opportunity.

A particularly appropriate analogous story, image, situation, or character can also simply maintain a presence in your script without taking over. It can appear as a recurring image—ominous, or humorous, or both! In Bill Irwin's hilarious play *The Regard of Flight*, the central character is compelled by a pushy critic and a stage manager/musician to define the "New Theatre." He struggles to demonstrate it, to rise above the "cheap devices" and "empty polish" of the "bourgeois theatre." Meanwhile, he is surrounded by many elements of that traditional theatre, including a proscenium that time and again malevolently and comically tries to swallow him up when he approaches it too closely.[19]

Different characters in separate segments or a set of characters may find continuity by continually meeting up with a consistent evocative image such as Irwin's proscenium. In a lighter vein, this is called a running gag. Each time the image appears, it helps anchor that moment within the context of the whole. And that, after all, is the purpose of a unifying image.

Along with recurring visual motifs, a sense of unity can be created by repeated use of musical motifs. *Evita* and *Les Misérables* are just two examples of world-renowned theatrical productions that repeatedly introduce fresh or only slightly altered lyrics to the same few musical compositions throughout their scores.

Music-Based Structures

The Open Theater, under the direction of Joseph Chaikin, counted among its many innovations the use of music's structures as models or inspirations for the structure of plays. In her enlightening book on Chaikin's work, Eileen Blumenthall describes Chaikin's belief that plays "can be built through the development and interweaving of themes and motifs. It is possible in this way to draw connections more complex and fragile than those of narrative or logic. . . . His basic principle in assembling a performance piece is not to construct a coherent story, but to find 'a shape that is musically tenable.' "[20]

To better understand how this might work, consider the structure of a piece of music such as Beethoven's Fifth Symphony. It starts with four notes, an initial, melodic fragment: ba ba ba bom. The fragment then repeats, but with a slight variation: ba ba ba bom. It then repeats over and over again, each time with more variation, contrast, and elaboration. There is no reason that a play can't be organized in the same way.

Determine which of the pieces are essentially variations on others and organize them so they progress in the way a piece of music progresses, by establishing a basic fragment and then showing the same thing with variations, contrasts, and elaborations. Has the cast created a scene, a choreographed dance, and a monologue that are all essentially about the same thing? Integrate some common visual or aural clues in all three so it becomes clear that each one is elaborating on the previous one. In music, patterns and rhythms set up expectations so the listener anticipates hearing a transition or a resolution. Similar patterns can be established in the staging of separate pieces. Reprises and codas bring listeners back to where the music began. The sequence of pieces in a show can be organized in the same way with the repetition of an opening motif. For those with an interest in or understanding of musical forms, it can be a challenge to try to repudiate the logic of a narrative and to weave together the segments of a show according to the rules of musical composition.

So, in reviewing your material, do any obvious possibilities emerge?

> Narrative: Could a story be invented or is there a singularly apt story from one of the pieces that could be expanded and adapted to encompass the whole show?
>
> A Series of Episodes: Will a simple presentation of the pieces be enough?
>
> Place: Is there a locale or environment where all the pieces could conceivably take place?
>
> A Prop: Is there an object or objects that could carry over from one segment to the next?
>
> Music-Based Structure: Is the assortment of pieces best suited to a structure inspired by music's forms, emphasizing recurring patterns and contrasts over plot?

There may, in fact, be several directions in which you can go. Try them all! Working individually, in groups, or with partners, the actors can devise some different scenarios employing some of the structures suggested here or any other structures they can think of.

Storyboards

As an alternative to writing out scenarios, try having the actors draw up outlines in storyboard form. This form is commonly used to present story outlines by professionals in the film and television industry. Storyboards show a progression of square or rectangular frames. In each frame is a simple drawing. It illustrates who is in the scene, where they are in relation to one another, and what they're doing. The frames will often have captions to help explain what's going on. When viewed together, the drawings graphically demonstrate what happens from one point to the next, how characters move from point A to point B to point C. These comic book versions of a script can be sketched out relatively quickly and then easily compared. They don't need to be works of art; stick figures are fine. If some individuals in the group invest a lot of time and effort in their storyboards, they may become rather attached to them and then be reluctant to compromise their plans. At this point, the ideas are still flying around fast and furious and the storyboards are only meant as a means to share ideas. Later, once the group decides on a structure everyone likes, people can create a more detailed storyboard. Along with more considered images of the stage pictures, it can feature notes about the intent of each scene, definitions of the specific turning points and transitions, and descriptions of the different layers: the underscoring music, text, sound, and so on.

If the group still feels stuck, consider either or both of the following approaches.

Sorting by Beginnings/Middles/Endings Separate the pieces into categories—beginnings, middles, and endings. For the beginnings, decide which of the pieces best establish and define the theme. Which ones will give the audience an overall impression of what the show is about? Which ones say, "This is what we're dealing with"?

Next, identify which pieces are about people's response to this issue. For the middles, consider those which show how people react to the issue in different ways. Which ones say, "This what people do in response"?

Finally, decide which pieces characterize where our behavior leads. Which ones show the options that our actions and choices leave us? Which ones show the directions we can go?

Now look again to see if there is something that can tie the segments together and propel them along.

Sorting by Contrasts Discuss some of the things the cast has learned about the subject of the show over the course of the workshops. (You may find it helpful at this time to return to the Questions worksheet, p. 35)

Then, as a group, identify one or more pairs of words or concepts that reflect the contrasts associated with this subject: how relationships, attitudes, or behaviors change or are different from one person to the next. Make a list of the contrasts, separating them with a slash. For example:

intimidated/confident
hopeful/hopeless
alone/surrounded by family and friends
given respect/disrespected
trapped/free

Now return to your abbreviated descriptions of each piece and see if they can be organized so as to describe an arc between the contrasts you have identified. Which ones exemplify the relationships, attitudes, or behaviors on one side of the slash, which ones match those on the other side, and which ones reveal how we move from one to the other?

OPENINGS

The first few moments of the show establish the world of the play and invite in the audience. Openings are critical. The audience's initial impression quite literally sets the stage for how it will respond to the rest of the show. If you can start with an opening that truly intrigues the audience members and captures their imaginations, you're on your way to a successful audience-actor interaction.

It's been said there are two ways to start off in street theatre: with a fanfare, which has to be done marvelously, or respectfully, demanding no response.[21] I generally choose between one of those two options. The musical *Sarafina!*, about children and the liberation of South Africa, begins with a fanfare. Dozens of schoolkids exuberantly burst upon the scene all at once and start singing the brassy opening song about their homeland. It is dazzling and impressive and it sweeps the audience along with its energy. In contrast, a show can open respectfully, gradually drawing the audience in. Enrique Vargas has described what actors can learn from an evangelical or Pentecostal church service. In the church, he says, "They usually begin with singing, movement, sound. The preachers know when the right time has come; the people begin to say 'Amen' together. This never happens at the beginning—they warm up. They're going to make something happen with their universe. It's done in complete connection with the congregation—and this is what theater is all about."[22] He was describing the larger picture of a theatre's relationship with its community, but his observations also hold true for the opening of a play. A single voice speaking, singing a simple song, or offering a single image or sound can gracefully build to a wealth of voices, enfolding the energies of the audience at the same time. Or that single voice can, by itself, introduce the audience to the world of the play.

FIRST ACT ENDINGS

If you choose to create a show with an intermission, it is customary to close the first act with something hanging in the balance. The first act ending is a transitional point that leaves the audience with a question, which presumably will be resolved in the second half. Although it is more obvious how to accomplish this with a narrative-based script, it can work just as successfully with alternative structures.

It may be obvious where to put the intermission. If, in the first part of the show, you've chosen to establish the issue and demonstrate how people respond to it, you may find there is one piece that, more than the others, represents the most critical aspect of how the issue impacts people's lives. Does one piece represent the most severe consequences of the ways in which people deal with this issue? These kinds of pieces implicitly ask the question, where do we go from here? Lead up to that moment, and then take your pause. The audience will want to come back to see where you're going with it. For example, a show about suicide might present a range of individuals all facing different kinds of risk factors. Throughout the course of the first act, we get to know them and see in each case how these factors can accumulate to the point at which a person considers ending his life. The first half could end with a piece reflecting the sense of desperation that comes when a number of risk factors all stack up. That is where you could place the intermission. The second half shows what happens next. In the second half, the pieces reveal what the actors believe help contribute to a person stepping away from suicide or going ahead with it. The show might conclude with pieces about the repercussions of a suicide for family and friends.

Alternatively, the two acts may work in counterpoint. For example, a show about teenage eating disorders might focus in the first half on the public persona of a popular girl. All the pieces could reveal her as bright and likeable, the image of perfection to her friends and family. There may be a few clues along the way that suddenly make sense when, just before intermission, she takes out a spoon and slips off to the bathroom to purge. The second act could focus on her private persona, her bulimia, her fears and feelings of self-contempt—the hidden side of trying to keep up with that public image.

Or, a script about ecological issues might show the journey from a passionate childhood concern for the environment to a jaded loss of faith that anything can be done to help the planet. The entire show might be built around that turning point between caring and not caring. The first act could lead up to that turning point and the second act could deal with the personal and public manifestations of a loss of hope. Or the first half could show the entire arc and the second half could show what it takes to draw a person back to caring. In either case, the end of the first half leaves the audience wondering what will happen next.

FINALES

Even when a production deals with a dire theme, the actors will generally be able to seize upon some aspect of it that offers a glimmer of hope. The finale is a good place to put it. Certainly the actors should discuss what they want to have their audience leave the theatre thinking or feeling, but they can also reflect upon what would get *them* to think or feel that way if they were in the audience. You can help the cast members tap into their best instincts by asking them to gauge whether there is one piece in their repertoire that, more than the others, gives *them* courage, instills faith, or inspires *them* to rededicate themselves to the challenge ahead.

A finale can work as a coda, returning to something from earlier in the show but with a new emphasis. There is a fine old tradition in both theatre and literature of concluding by returning full circle to some element introduced in the beginning, now seen in a different light. Take a look to see if there is a strong piece that would take on new meaning if it were altered and rewoven into the script as a reprise.

If the group hasn't created a piece that fits the bill, design one now! By this time the cast is accustomed to experimenting with imagery to find what packs the most theatrical wallop. The actors can share some stories about what in their experiences has served to galvanize their own spirits. They can unpack those stories and use the elements they find to shape a powerful finale.

5 REHEARSING AND PERFORMING

A skilled director's sentences are questions. "How could we improve this? How could we clarify this? How could we get across the idea that she is looking for help? How could we simplify this entrance? Where has he come from? What does she have in mind? What is the objective in this scene? Could we try this again? Could we upgrade the objective? Could we pick up the pace?"
William Ball

This section could be subtitled "A Few Notes on Directing," since there is really room here for only a handful of suggestions. Given the limitations, the discussion will center on a little practical information about planning rehearsals and on some of the techniques I've found most effective for coaching actors and designing stage pictures. Along the way, I'll refer the reader to the books on directing that I have found to be especially helpful.

PREPARING FOR REHEARSALS

That stack of papers in front of you is now in provisional sequence with notes about transitions. Someone must be entrusted to patch it all together into one manageable script with clean, organized pages. More often than not, the task falls to the director. Besides typing up the script or cutting and pasting it on a word processor, there are some organizational duties ahead, including laying out a plan for rehearsals. Whoever is responsible for the composition of the songs and incidental music must finish up the work and make preparations to teach it to the actors and musicians; this may or may not involve writing out sheet music. If you have included borrowed or adapted work, take time to confirm that permission has been granted where appropriate. And, depending upon the scale of the production you are planning, it's time to start work on costume/scene design and on publicizing the show now that there is a relatively secure sense of the script.

Casting

Casting is never easy. It's always a challenge to strike a balance between what individuals can do and what will challenge them. Ideally, the actors should all be cast in roles that will let them shine, roles that will showcase their talents. In some cases, you can give the actors an opportunity to audition for roles under contention, although a director who has worked closely with them as they developed their script may not need to hold traditional tryouts. If a musical director has been working with the group, he or she will know who is capable of singing which song or whether a song can be adjusted to accommodate a specific singer.

Many of the actors will have their eyes on specific parts they'd like to play. Sometimes I've had actors submit their personal wish lists, and I've also occasionally asked each one to be the casting director for the entire company. They have had a chance to get to know one another pretty well. I make a list of all the parts in all the pieces and have each individual write down who she thinks would be best for each role, song, and choreography. This may not work for the chronically self-absorbed but, in general, it can encourage the actors to consider how they fit into the whole ensemble and what casting would best serve the show. The director can look at each wish list or casting sheet, make a master list reflecting preferences and suggestions, and take all the information under advisement. If an individual actor was largely responsible for developing a particular piece or is the only one with a skill needed for a certain role, that may also play a part in the casting decision.

Music

A group that has chosen to incorporate music and song into its show may be relying on a staff musical director/composer. If not, individual cast members may possess the skill and inclination to compose and perform the show's music themselves. Or there may be a composer and musicians on the periphery, friends of cast members or the director who can be drafted for the job. The group may look to an amateur neighborhood band or, in schools fortunate enough to have a music department, some of the more talented students in band class. Whether you have on staff a professional composer and musicians or have found a few volunteers with a gift for music and time to contribute, the task is the same. They must take the lyrics the cast has developed and fit them to tunes that reflect their spirit.

The instrumentation can be performed live, integrated into the show on stage or to the side. It is also possible to prerecord the music so that the singers are accompanied on audiotape. Live music can be very exciting, but there is also something to be said for taped orchestration. A group of professional musicians may be willing to commit to a one-time rehearsal and recording session but not to a whole run of performances. If they can be brought on board to make a sound tape, their work can set a high standard that can upgrade the quality of the singers' performances and the overall quality of the show. And, of course, there is no reason that a performance can't include a combination of both live and prerecorded music.

Scheduling Rehearsals

The script should be divided into working units and then plotted on a calendar so each unit receives repeated opportunities for rehearsal. Working units are sections of the script that involve a set number of actors. A working unit may be an entire song, monologue, or scene or just some of its elements. For example, if a scene will ultimately be performed with musical or vocal underscoring, the scene would be one working unit involving a few actors. The vocal underscoring would be another working unit involving the singers. Initially they should be rehearsed separately. When both are strong, you can integrate the rehearsals. A long scene may be broken into smaller working units divided according to logical breaks: the entrance of new characters, interruptions, and so on. Gradually the rehearsals will integrate the separate elements of each piece and will start stringing together successive chunks of working units. Closer to the end of rehearsals, schedule complete run-throughs. Some eleventh-hour rehearsal times labeled TBA for "to be announced" allow for a little flexibility if it becomes apparent that particular units need extra work.

The first rehearsal will be a time for checking in with one another, looking over the plans for the set and costumes, reading through the whole script, and hearing the music for the songs. Subsequent rehearsals should, like the script development workshops, incorporate a little time at the start for physical and vocal warm-ups. Actors in some groups may possess the initiative and discipline to warm up on their own or with one another as they arrive. Other groups may require a more formally led company warm-up.

The Changing Role of the Director

As you prepare to begin rehearsals, it is important to adjust for a difference in the relationship between the director and the actors. Much has been made in earlier sections about the collaborative nature of building the script. A subtle shift is about to take place. The group is about to move from a participatory democracy to a representative democracy with you, the director, representing their interests. There is still plenty of room for your constituency to contribute ideas and assessments about the direction of the show but, from now on, cast members need to channel their suggestions through you. Rehearsals will grind to a halt if actors start pitching contradictory suggestions to their fellow cast members or take turns coaching one another on the side. It's tough enough for actors to make confident decisions about acting and staging choices with just one director giving them feedback. If they have to contend with a roomful of directors, each advocating a different opinion, it can be overwhelming.

You can make it clear that you are always available to consider everyone's point of view. There can be regular opportunities for gathering to talk about how it's going and you can encourage actors to take you aside to offer their views. But from here on out, the cast members will have to trust you to represent their best interests and the best interests of the show. If all has gone according to plan, they will trust you. Still, it may be difficult for some to relinquish the egalitarianism to which they've become accustomed. With this in mind, it is not a bad idea to anticipate the transition. As early as the start of the project, or as late as the end of the script development phase, you can talk to them about the ways in which the actor-director relationship will change when rehearsals begin.

COACHING THE ACTORS

Actions and Objectives

The cast members have worked hard to create a script that illuminates their perspectives about something they believe is important. They have a vision of what they want to communicate. But they may still be thinking as playwrights. To help them transform their passion for the issue into a passionate performance, the director can serve them best by helping them find something specific that they can *do* on stage.

I'm always willing to sacrifice a certain degree of subtlety in character development when directing cast-generated shows on topical issues. Rather than have actors spend hours fleshing out details about their characters' personal history, habits, and memories, I have them use the typically limited amount of time to get right to the point. What do their characters want and how are they going to get it? Having created their own script, the cast members know what their characters want. The challenge is to get them to express what that is in a form that will bring their performances to life: to express it in the form of a verb, sometimes called an *actable verb*. Unlike an adjective (he's a *funny* kid), or a noun (he's *the class clown*), an actable verb gives the performer something he wants to *do* (he wants to *grab* everyone's attention; to *captivate* the girls; to *crack up* the boys; to *provoke* his teacher; to *test* how much he can get away with; to *win* everybody's affection). All those verbs give him specific actions he can carry out in order to obtain his objective. This simple adjustment makes a tremendous difference in the strength of an actor's performance. Consideration of actions and objectives is the legacy of the Russian theatre director and teacher Konstantin Stanislavski. In my opinion, the best contemporary presentation of Stanislavski's method, as far as directors are concerned, can be found in Bill Ball's marvelous book *A Sense of Direction: Some Observations on the Art of Directing*.[23]

If you are not familiar with it already, track down a copy. It offers a wealth of valuable insight for directors, expressed in a very practical manner.

Working primarily with untrained actors, I have made much use of what Ball calls "the crowbars" of directing. Just as a crowbar can be relied upon to crudely but effectively get the job done, he proposes two variations on a simple question for actors that will quickly get to the heart of what they're doing on stage:

> What are you trying to *get* him [her] to do?
> What are you trying to *make* him [her] do?

The crowbar questions are especially useful because, since they explicitly state a specific desired response, they compel each actor to relate to the others. For example, a character in one scene may want to be the self-appointed leader of a group. Instead of acting or being domineering in a general way, she is trying to get everyone to quiet down and listen to her. The actor can latch on to that objective and pursue it with single-minded ferocity. Everything she does involves connecting with the other actors. She doesn't stop until she gets what she wants or until something else happens that changes the situation. (The actors know where those turning points are; they built them into the script themselves.) As for the other characters, what are their objectives? Instead of acting vaguely intimidated, they are actively trying to make her listen to reason. The actors have supplied themselves with words and gestures that reflect their characters' behavior, but the crowbar questions help them anchor those words and gestures with concrete actions.

Beyond *get* and *make*, you can encourage the actors to identify verbs that allow for more subtle shades of intent. For example, the actor playing the domineering person described previously may decide that instead of just getting the others to shut up, her character is going to *terrify* them into submission or *make* them give in. Perhaps she is going to *take control* or *get* them to obey her. By precisely identifying what her character is trying to do at every moment and using her words and gestures as a means of making it happen, her performance becomes engaged.

In *A Sense of Direction*, Ball shows that not all verbs are equal. Some verbs are easier than others to sink one's teeth into. He submits that a great deal of the director's job in rehearsal is first to make sure the actors have picked verbs they can try out and then, where appropriate, to help them upgrade their verbs. That is to say, the director works with the actors to come up with modifications on those verbs that make them more *actable*: more forceful or less abstract. A more actable verb will lead to a more vivid performance.

When assisting actors in upgrading their verb choices, it can be useful to have a thesaurus on hand or to encourage the actors to make use of one. Some verb may seem just perfect to you because of a personal association but doesn't mean much to the actor. It fails to capture his imagination. You can use a thesaurus like a foreign language phrasebook to help find a related or synonymous verb that strikes a chord for the actor. For example, "I want him to give me some space" might work fine for the director, but the actor might have more success with "I want him to back off!"

Another helpful source is Michael Shurtleff's fine book *Audition: Everything an Actor Needs to Know to Get the Part*. Although ostensibly about auditioning, the book contains first-rate advice that is fully applicable to preparing a role for performance. His "Twelve Guideposts" is a succinct checklist that can help inexperienced actors vastly improve their work on stage. I particularly appreciate his take on getting actors to state their objectives. To ensure they make a strong choice, he avoids talk of goals or motivation or wants or verbs. Rather, he asks them, "What are you fighting for?"[24]

Rehearsal is the place where actors can try out various verbs for effectiveness. From one session to the next, the actors will test, discard, replace, adjust, and upgrade their verb choices. A standard part of the actors' equipment should be a pencil, which they can use to write down in the margins of their scripts what they're fighting for or what specifically they're trying to get someone to do at each moment they're on stage. Pencil is better than pen to allow for discoveries and changes according to what works best. The workshop journals can now be pressed into service as rehearsal notebooks. A part of the actors' preparatory homework can be to come up with a list of possible verbs to bring to rehearsal to try out. The notebook is a fine place to write down ideas. Along with potential verbs, the actors can note their ideas for gests (gestures, pauses, stresses, etc.) and their thoughts about where the gests might come into play.

Rehearsal is also the place where the director and cast can flesh out stage business. It may be that the script development workshop sessions have produced various notes in the script that read, "comedy routine with hats here," or, "choreography about saying goodbye here with these gestures," followed by some sketches. Rehearsal is the appropriate place to work out the specifics of those physical actions, along with the general movement (blocking) and transitions. More often than not, working out solutions to blocking and transitions is simply a matter of finding the most interesting and theatrically legitimate way to solve problems.

Alternate Futures

Along with having them write down what they're fighting for or what they're trying to get or make the other characters do, ask the actors to imagine and then write down how their *characters* think a situation is going to turn out at each of the turning points in the script. For example, to return again to the domineering character, the script may show that eight lines into her dialogue she will be stopped in her bid to take control of the room. Something will happen that changes everything and the whole group will start to ridicule her. Knowing the way the scene plays out, the actor might anticipate the turning point and hold herself back just a little. Encourage her to ignore what the script says, imagine the situation the way her character thinks it's going to turn out, and play the scene as if it's going to go that way. She'll picture what it's going to look like when she succeeds. She'll picture all the others sitting down in neat rows listening to her instructions and obeying her commands. When she plays the scene with this image squarely in her head, she'll be that much more committed to making it happen. And when the plot turns, the juncture will be that much more apparent. The reason this is useful, aside from encouraging the actors to fully commit to their actions, is that it heightens their attention to the moment of change. When they have expressly clarified for themselves how and when a situation that's heading one direction is altered by some specific event or choice, those in the audience become more aware of it too.[25]

Epic Acting

One of the things Brecht wrote a great deal about was an approach to performing that he called an epic acting style. *Epic acting* is intended to encourage the audience always to remain conscious that the actor is an actor and not the character she is portraying. It is generally considered high praise when someone tells an actor, "You had me convinced; I really thought you were that character." Actors are trained to slip into the skin of the role, to try to embody a character and create the illusion of verisimilitude for the audience. But the actor's emphasis on working to express the character's inner feelings will encourage the audience to share in those feelings vicariously. There is a great risk, especially when presenting material dealing with substantive social issues, that an audience will get caught up in the character's feelings and will miss out on the meaning of the scene.

Let me give an example. One of the most powerful performances I've ever seen on stage was by an adolescent in a production of Elizabeth Swados' play *Runaways*. The monologue is called "I Went Back Home." It is a very painful story. A girl tells of living on the streets and then returning home only to be met by horrendous verbal and physical abuse from her family. The performer was very talented and deeply authentic in her portrayal. Sitting in the audience, I found it very difficult to take. She was so believable that it absolutely seemed like her own testimonial, as if she were a ringer among a group of actors playing runaway kids. I shifted uneasily between two worlds. One moment I was drawn into severe feelings of distress and revulsion over what she had gone through; I switched into parent/protector mode and wondered what I could do to help this child. The next moment I was consciously pulling back, reminding myself it was only a play and that this kid was certainly doing an impressive acting job. Between intense concern over the welfare of that particular girl on the stage and a sort of clinical withdrawal for the sake of my own emotional self-preservation, I missed the big picture. Oh, I had a fulfilling theatrical experience, and I enthusiastically applauded her work during the curtain call. But as far as gaining a deeper appreciation of the situation, I was too caught up to notice. What I got was "The experience of abuse is painful." What I would have liked to have gotten was "How is one led into being abused?" and "How does one discover a way out?"

How could the actor have shown me the anguish of that girl in such a way that I would have been neither so overwhelmed nor so detached? What could she have done differently to get me to see what was happening with a clearheaded compassion? Brecht maintained that it comes down to her intent as a performer. If she sees her task as embodying the emotions of her character, the audience may well find her believable and be swept along. For many actors, including young actors, this is exactly what makes performing fun. One gets to leave the mundane behind and *affect* the emotions of someone else. However, if her intent is to clearly and consciously show the audience what this girl is going through, she can use her voice, her body, and her props to emphasize the *effects* of her character's social situation.

Brecht's wonderfully simple illustration is that of an eyewitness demonstrating to a crowd of bystanders what has just happened in a traffic accident. Some of the people in the crowd didn't see what happened. Others saw it but have different opinions about who was at fault. The eyewitness shows the way he saw it. He demonstrates the way the pedestrian was walking, clearly thinking of something other than the curb. He demonstrates how the truck driver's hair was messed up, in the manner of someone groggy with lack of sleep. Or he shows exactly how the driver's arm was wrapped around the young woman there in the passenger seat, his attention devoted to her. The eyewitness is not reproducing everything in the scene as realistically as possible. He is selecting out what is significant and capturing it precisely. With his physical bearing, gestures, and tone of voice, he is artfully showing what he believes made the accident inevitable and how, under different circumstances, it might have been avoided.

He's not trying to cast a spell over the rest of the crowd, to convince them he is the pedestrian or the truck driver. But through his actions he has created a full picture of the event. Brecht admits this is a primitive model. He acknowledges the stage performance of an epic actor will be richer, much more intricate and complex. But he insists this basic attitude of the actor toward the material is what separates the epic actor's work from the traditional dramatic actor's. The actor's subtle shift from becoming possessed by a character to representing a character shifts the attention of the audience. Instead of seducing the observers into feeling what the character feels, the actor puts their focus on what is happening. The scenes highlight the characters' relationships, what led up to these circumstances, and where the alternatives lie.[26]

I have found young actors can pretty easily begin to understand an epic acting style just by listening to Brecht's example of the eyewitness at the street scene. Describe the example to them and suggest that this approach to acting is as if they were being asked to impersonate people, not making fun of them in an exaggerated way, but precisely to reproduce what they do: their gestures, tone of voice, the way they walk, the way they behave. Ask them if they know someone who is really good at mimicking people, or if any of them is good at it. If there are some volunteers, have them try to "do" one another or their director, not cruelly, but accurately. Have everyone look at their demonstrations and discuss what makes a good mimic appealing or funny or enlightening. It usually succeeds when the impersonator is right on target. He's selected a couple of things that precisely capture some of the physical qualities and contradictions of another person. If a mimic can "do" another person without malice or even parody but with a sense of three-dimensionality, it can be extremely captivating. We in the audience start to notice details about the person being imitated that we may not have noticed before. That alone, you can suggest, is enough to make good theatre. What's more, the mimic can show us someone going through a highly emotional time, but the audience never becomes overwhelmed with concern for the mimic himself. By allowing the audience to watch the experience one step removed, actors allow the audience to see what's happening to the character with clearer eyes.

So the task of acting is redefined. Rather than dwelling exclusively on their characters' inner psychology, the actors spend their time working out what they can do physically to reveal their characters' attitudes and relationships. In fact, the actors already have a head start on identifying these elements; they've been an integral part of their script from the outset. In rehearsals, they test out their choices for clarity. They refine and improve them. They add to them. They reject the choices that turn out to be vague or clichéd. The actors still identify what their characters are fighting for (verbs) and what they expect to have happen (alternate futures) and they play those actions fully. But their attitude is different. Instead of trying to convince themselves and their audience that their characters' wants are their own, they always remain aware that as actors, they are demonstrating to the audience exactly how these characters pursue their wants. In performance, they won't need literally or figuratively to wink at their audience to indicate that they're not really these characters. It will come across in clear but subtle ways. Instead of putting their energy into evoking a wash of feelings, the actors will be paying attention to the pauses, the small gestures, the changes in voice, the ways in which they use their lines, and the responses to others that clarify what's going on from moment to moment. The audience will see these things and, if they ring true, will respond to them. The scene will be about those moments and social interactions instead of about the emotions of the characters.

This approach may also provide a safe way in for some cast members. Performing a role puts a person in a vulnerable position. Participants with no qualms about showing off in front of others may be reluctant to take the risk of becoming a character. These individuals may be much more willing to commit to imitating what someone does—how he behaves. It allows them a little distance from that vulnerability. You can encourage these actors to think of it as being a member of a sports team working to improve accuracy in hitting the ball or making the shot. In this case, you can challenge them to become more accurate and more precise in their observation and impersonation skills. What needs to be adjusted for the actor to get the imitation right on target?

An exciting side effect of this approach is that it tends to promote an emphasis on ensemble work rather than on solo achievement. Instead of becoming wrapped up in expressing the drama or comedy of their individual roles, the actors become interested in how their choices mesh with their fellow actors. The challenge quickly becomes focused on whether the collective interaction, the reactions and responses, is correctly communicating the intent of the piece.

Throughout the rehearsal process, you can frame your feedback according to what is coming across. You can report: "This is what I'm getting—is this what we want? Are the clues clear? How can we show it best?" Rather than asking the actors to make their characters more realistic, you can encourage them to be clearer and to let go of choices that aren't working. It can be thrilling when the cast finds those elements that truly capture the sense of characters or situations. The whole group will spot it when an impersonation or interaction is unmistakably accurate. A collective gasp or the laughter of recognition is the ultimate sign that you've got something that works.

Verfremdungseffekt

In addition to the actors' attitude that they are demonstrating rather than becoming their characters, it is possible to incorporate other elements into the performance that derail the audience's natural tendency to become caught up in the emotions of the scene. Brecht was known for integrating techniques, devices, and effects into the staging of his plays that did just that. He used the marvelous-sounding *verfremdungseffekt* to describe this. It has been awkwardly translated into English as *alienation effect*. A more direct translation would be *strange-making effect*, which gets to the heart of his intent. When we see something strange, when there is something markedly out of the ordinary about what would otherwise be an ordinary incident, we look at it more carefully. The same is true of the reverse: when something we're not used to seeing is presented as something familiar, we go from being passive to alert. We ask, "What's going on here? What does it mean?" We see it in a fresh way. For example, the fact that one character continually avoids taking responsibility might just be taken for granted by the audience. However, if the cast wanted to emphasize his behavior, the actors could make it a little more unusual: every time he slips away, he slips away on a trapeze or a pogo stick.[27]

These verfremdungseffekts (V-effects) can also help stop the audience members from becoming so concerned for the characters' well-being that they lose track of what the characters are doing. Imagine a scene in which a harsh interrogation is used as an obvious metaphor for a certain kind of relationship. Even if it is played in an exaggerated fashion, it will still lead some in the audience to feel some pity or fear for the victim. But, by having the same actor play both accused and accuser, jumping back and forth between sitting in the hot seat and looming over it, the actor allows feelings of pity or fear to melt away. The scene becomes comic and serious at the same time and the audience watches what happens.

Or, imagine the police are on their way to capture the protagonist. The audience would ordinarily be caught up in suspense, wondering whether or not the protagonist is going to escape in time. But if the scene began with a sign that read, "At the end of this scene, he'll be caught and put in jail," the suspense would be deflated. The observers would know what is going to happen so, instead, they would find themselves watching *how* it happens.[28]

In order to help them clarify their epic acting sense of separation from the character, Brecht occasionally asked his actors to transpose their lines from first to third person during rehearsal. I have had success with this not just as a rehearsal technique, but in performance, too, using it as a V-effect. In the previous section, I described a monologue about a young woman named Barbara Johns whose dedication led her to play an important part in the American Civil Rights movement. The story was borrowed from a lecture given by the writer Juan Williams. He naturally told the story in the third person. He began by saying, extemporaneously:

> Barbara Johns was sixteen years old and attending a segregated school in Prince Edward County, Virginia. Now when I say segregated, I don't mean it was a school that just had Blacks in it. It was a bunch of shacks put together with a tar paper roof, and no floor—just dirt. And when the rains would come, the floors would become thick with mud. That was the school. In fact, the Black students could only go to school in November, December, January, and February, months when there weren't crops to be put in the ground or crops to be harvested. This was the reality of school for Black children. And she went home and said to her parents, "You know, it's wrong. The White kids get to go off to these brick buildings, with new books. It's wrong. I don't wanna just be a farmer's wife."[29]

The teenager who performed that piece in our show would herself have made a convincing Barbara Johns. But rather than adapting the speech into first person as a testimonial-style monologue, we kept it in the third person. When speaking Barbara's words, the actor was able to be passionate while obviously never pretending to be her. In the descriptive passages, the actor's own attitude about what had happened came through in Juan Williams' words. For example, here are the last few sentences:

> And when people talk about *Brown versus Board of Education*, the tendency is to think about Thurgood Marshall; the tendency is to think about Earl Warren. But, for me, it boils down to that young woman, Barbara Johns, who at sixteen was willing to stand up for

something, willing to believe in it, willing to work at it, and never, never give up.[30]

The impact of the speech was startling. Instead of being caught up in seeing the actor on stage as a dramatic reincarnation of the real Barbara Johns and cheering her on personally, many audience members reported later that they found themselves gripped by what Barbara had accomplished. Their attention was on how she faced her struggle—what she went through and what it took for her to succeed. The young actor was able to assume Barbara's persona with an assurance that was truly captivating but, by performing the story in the third person, she was able also to present the character's behavior and relationships as separate from herself.

An inventive ensemble can devise any number of variations to achieve the same kind of V-effect as transposition to third person. If the intent is to make it clear that the actors aren't the roles they're playing, they can experiment with performing roles for which they are clearly ill-suited. A female can play the role of a male talking about women. A seventeen-year-old can play the role of a fifty-year-old talking about teenagers. Or, for those with a flair for fun, eleven-year-olds can ride on the shoulders of other eleven-year-olds and, with the help of a long dress and a long trenchcoat, the ones on top can play two adults talking about eleven-year-olds. These performances need not be parodies! The actors can be scrupulously attentive about creating well-defined characters. Beyond these kinds of reversals, consider other ways to help the audience connect with what is happening instead of becoming swept away by the personalities of the characters. Several actors, dressed in identical costumes, might all play the same person, trading off from scene to scene. The realistic dialogue of a scene or the lines of a monologue might be turned into a song or rhyme to help keep it from being so believably realistic. A highly charged emotional scene might be performed silently while an observer who cares about those involved tells the audience what's going on. It can be a fun challenge. What can you adjust to cause the audience to see a familiar situation in a strange way or to see something they're not accustomed to seeing in a way that makes it familiar?[31]

Don't worry that the audience will be less affected by the power of a performance in which the realism is derailed. In 1929, Brecht produced his play *The Baden-Baden Cantata of Acquiescence*. It featured a clown with extended wooden legs and arms and a large and obviously fake wooden head. There were two more human clowns with him and, after discussing man's inhumanity to man, the two began blithely to saw the legs off the puppet, to horrifying effect. According to historian John Fuegi, the fact that the violence was perpetrated on a puppet apparently did not detract at all from the power of the scene. The audience was deeply moved by this appalling act, perhaps even more than it would have been if a human clown had been attacked. In this production, the audience wasn't concerned with an actor being hurt, nor was it distracted by the spectacle of special-effect blood. Everyone was focused entirely on what was happening.[32]

The Thumb Trick

It is conventional wisdom that acting is reacting. However, during the first few weeks of rehearsals, when actors are still holding their scripts, it can be awfully difficult to get that re-acting engaged. There is a great tendency for them to keep their faces buried in the pages while delivering lines. It may actually be that the first time they see one anothers' eyes is after they've memorized their words and put away their scripts. The thumb trick is an old and deceptively simple technique that is especially useful for getting actors to start relating to one another early on in rehearsal.

The thumb trick simply refers to an actor holding a script so that his thumb is next to the line he's saying. As the scene progresses, he moves his thumb down as a placeholder. Now, when he looks up to deliver a line and then looks back at his script, he doesn't have to scan the whole page to figure out where he is. When rehearsing, an actor can look at his line and penciled-in margin notes, take it all in, then look up, connect with the other actor, and use that line to deliver the intent of the action. If he doesn't get the words exactly right, it's not a problem. They're just words. Eventually he'll memorize them but, for now, he's using rehearsal time to interact. And what a difference it makes! The other actor responds to what he's said, then glances at the place in her script where her thumb is, takes in the line and the notes, looks up, and gives her line back, also fully engaged. This is slower than the rapid-fire reading of dialogue. There are pauses between each line while the actors get a hook on the action behind what they're about to say or do, but it is worth the wait. Instead of just reading, the actors become engaged with one another and the rehearsals become much more productive.

Monologues

If the script calls for a monologue directed to the audience, an actor will be much better equipped to deliver it if he can come up with a very specific idea of whom his character is talking to and why. The monologue may never identify who his audience is, but that doesn't mean he can't make something up to help him focus his work. Even if those in the audience don't know who they're "supposed" to be, the fact that the actor has a specific relationship in mind will give them the feeling a relationship does exist. It will also give the actor something to work with. It is one thing to tell a story to a sea of anonymous theatregoers sitting in a dim auditorium. It is quite another to justify one's behavior to a panel of juvenile hall judges, to warn a younger brother with a cautionary story, or to try to impress older kids in a parking lot with tales of bravado. Working with the director, the actor can figure out a relationship that works best for the speech. Then he can look at the audience members and imagine them as the judges, the brother, or the parking lot crowd. What is his character fighting for? What specifically does he want to get from them? Acquittal? A promise? Acceptance? What does his character do physically to get what he wants? How does he adjust what he is saying according to whom he is talking? These kinds of questions will lead to a much more vivid performance than a speech aimed vaguely at the audience.

Songs

All the suggestions for delivering monologues or performing scenes apply just as well to singing songs. The singers can formulate a clear idea of what they're fighting for or what they're trying to make happen through the lyrics of their songs. If the song is directed to the audience, the singer can invent an appropriate identity for the listeners and sing to them with that relationship in mind. It is also possible for a performer to sing to herself. In *The Wizard of Oz*, when Dorothy sings "Somewhere Over the Rainbow," she's worried about old Miss Gulch, but no one will listen to her. In the song she tries to figure out what a place where there isn't any trouble would look like. By imagining it, she can bring herself some comfort. The singer could decide that, by singing the song, Dorothy is trying to make herself feel better or push her worries away.

Many young performers conceive of a song as just a series of stanzas, so they tend to drop their energy at the conclusion of each line. A clear sense of what their characters are fighting for in a song can help these singers keep tuned in even in the pauses between their singing.

Find the Love

One final word about coaching actors. The word is *love*. "Find the love" was a direction given to me as a student actor and it has served me well for many years as an actor and director. Hateful characters are not very appealing to an audience. Nor are characters who wallow in self-pity. They come across as simply objectionable and we often just wait for them to go away. A skilled actor will always find what his character loves and make that a part of what he's fighting for. Even a character who appears to hate everyone may in fact just passionately love her solitude and will do anything to keep it, including scaring people away. Always ask the actors to find the love in the piece and in the character. They'll be rewarded by an audience that is drawn to their work on stage and interested in seeing what happens to their characters.

STAGING

The cast members will have devised many ideas about staging and transitions between pieces as a part of developing the script. As the director, you can check to see if their ideas are in fact communicating the intent of each piece and, to keep it interesting, you can make sure the whole show incorporates variations in scale, pace, and rhythm. Don't be afraid to consult the actors for their opinions about what can be done to increase the tension of a scene, to improve a segue, or to make two contrasting scenes more distinct. You can also give them an opportunity to ask for your opinion by periodically inquiring whether there is anything they're having trouble with in a scene. Unless you ask, you may not realize they are struggling with something.

Variation will make the show more interesting. The use of different planes—from having actors on the ground, to standing on chairs, on platforms, or even on stilts—can create visual interest. Variation in scale and pace and rhythm may mean that a small and intimate scene is followed by a scene involving lots of actors filling the stage or that a frenetic comedy scene is followed by a gentler, more thoughtful one. Variation in scale may also mean that a scene with ordinary-sized actors is followed by a scene featuring a couple of oversized puppets or perhaps by a scene in which the characters are small found objects being manipulated by the performers. You can use music in many ways. A single tambourine or other instrument can increase the tension or perceived momentum of a piece. A recurring musical motif can help move the show from one piece to the next. Music can even be used in direct counterpoint for emphasis. Beautiful voices singing choir music could be layered over a piece about a painful experience.

The key to a successful transition lies in finding some logical reason for moving from point A to point B. Whether it is a gradual segue or a conscious interruption, something needs to occur on stage or off that alters the status quo and leads to the next moment. But there is more to staging than just adding visual and aural interest. It must reveal meaning; truly successful stage blocking will make a play comprehensible to a deaf audience, the physical action alone will communicate the relationships and the sense of what's going on.

On the subject of crafting clear and dynamic stage pictures, Bill Ball acknowledges the important lessons found in Chapters 7 and 8 of the book *Fundamentals of Play Directing* by Alexander Dean and Lawrence Carra.[33] He has great praise for what these two men have to teach directors. I absolutely agree and respectfully pass along his recommendation that aspiring directors take a look at that section of Dean and Carra's fine book.

PERFORMANCES

Warm-Ups

Just as the group took time for physical and vocal warm-ups at the start of each script development workshop session and rehearsal, build in an expectation that the cast members will warm up together before the performances. When setting the call time (the time when actors are scheduled to arrive), make sure to allow time for warming up. It may be there are songs from your score that would work well as preshow vocal warm-ups. If not, or if there are no songs in your show, seek out some that will. The benefits of a preshow warm-up extend beyond just limbering up voices and bodies so the cast will be ready for the physical requirements of the performance. The preshow warm-up is a valuable way for the group to leave the distractions of the day behind. It creates a break that allows actors to become present, to reconnect with one another, and to turn their attention to what is ahead.

Dedications

In his book *The Presence of the Actor*, Joseph Chaikin describes actors dedicating a performance. The idea is for the cast members to gather for a moment just prior to curtain time and decide upon someone to whom they will dedicate what they are about to do. It may be someone they admire. The person may be associated with the theme of the show or he or she may be someone to whom they feel a connection or relationship for some other reason. The subject of their dedication may be a group of people involved in a cause they believe in and wish to support. They select some person or persons and they verbally affirm together that they are going to play *this* performance for whomever it is they have chosen. It is a very simple thing. They fully understand that they may not always keep the dedication in mind when they are on stage. They may remember and forget through the course of the show. But they begin by making the gesture, the conscious decision to make this performance not only a gift to the audience but also a gift to a specific individual or group. The dedication helps them reconnect their performance with their original purpose in creating it. Instead of performing to please the audience, they perform because it's important to do. The whole cast may decide together to whom or what it wants to dedicate the performance, or each actor may choose separately and/or privately. In either case, the act of making a nightly dedication can serve to encourage and enliven the actors' passion about their work and their connection to the audience.[34]

Postperformance Dialogue

The group may choose to establish time for a postperformance dialogue with the audience. Spectators who don't wish to stay should be given a few minutes to slip out gracefully before it begins. Moderating a discussion like this is pretty straightforward. The cast sits on the stage. People in the auditorium with questions or comments raise their hands and a volunteer member of the cast acknowledges them in turn. Rather than conducting a formal actor-audience exchange, the cast members may want simply to be available for informal talk in the lobby after the show. Or they can create a comments book or have pieces of paper available for the audience to write upon.

Check-In Time

At a few points along the way in this process, the cast members have discussed what they will consider their measure of success. They can probably count on applause; there is truth in the cynical old saying that an audience will applaud a show even if it's good. But these actors haven't been working all this time for applause; they've been working for an opportunity to be heard. It doesn't hurt to clarify, once again, what they've hoped to accomplish with this project. Do they have a show they feel good about? Before each performance they can take a few minutes to check in with one another about the way the show is going and how they feel the audience has been responding.

Closure

After the final performance is complete, the set is struck, and the actors have had their cast party, it's always a good idea to gather for one last time to reflect upon the whole process. It will have been an intense time of passions and joy, flaring tempers, frustrations, and great fun. If nothing else, a closure meeting allows the participants to say goodbye to all they've gone through together, rather than just casually drifting away.

TO THE READER

One final thought in closing: Never lose faith that the work you are doing is worth all the effort it takes. By helping young people turn their energies and passions into art, you are providing an enormously valuable service, both for them and for the larger community. Whether or not they go on to pursue theatre in their lives, you will have taught these young people that their voices are important and that they have the power to make themselves heard. And here I will let the social anthropologist Ruthanne Kurth-Schai have the last word.

> The imaginative experiences of childhood represent humanity's primary source of personal and cultural evolutionary potential. [Youth possess the capacity] to create images of the future powerful enough to guide and motivate positive social change . . . In a world characterized by widespread feelings of purposelessness and powerlessness, the social contributions of childhood represent a primary source of humanity's hope for the future.[35]

APPENDIX A
Tools

The following list is meant only as a rough starting point for gathering tools. The world is full of debris and I never cease to be amazed at how the most common objects can be used to vividly evoke relationships and situations both dramatic and comic. If anything, the ease of accumulating stuff leads to a problem of storage. To save on space, a group may want to start a Spur Book. It is a handmade catalog of images that supplements some of the tools in one's collection. Over time, the actors bring in pictures cut from magazines, photocopied from books, and so on. They then paste or tape these pictures of objects of every kind, big and small, to the pages of a notebook. Now, along with looking over the assembled pile of actual tools to spur their imaginations, the actors can look over a wide assortment of pictures. When they find something that's perfect for a piece they're creating, they can go in search of it. Along with pictures of objects, the Spur Book can include the titles and descriptions of stories categorized by function the way Vladimir Propp categorized Russian folktales. The actors can create headings such as "stories about people by themselves," "stories about fights," "stories about helpers," and "stories about solving problems." The same categories can, of course, include songs and poems, too. The Spur Book will grow and become a valuable resource for continued theatre making. In the meantime, here are a few suggestions to start you gathering.

Kinetic

- beanbags
- dolly or rolling cart of some kind
- skateboard
- foam rubber balls
- silk or rayon scarves
- balloons
- gymnastic mats for tumbling and physical work
- knee and elbow pads

Height

stepladder
stilts
overturned buckets and cans
table and chairs
wooden boxes and milk crates

Light and Shadow

flashlights
halogen lamp for use with a shadow screen (Be careful, they get hot!)
a large piece of white fabric for use as a shadow screen

Sound

sticks and blocks
triangle
bells of all kinds
tambourine
cymbal
kalimba (African thumb piano)
drums (Any kind of can can be inverted and drummed upon.)
plastic tubes that can be made into hornlike wind instruments
penny whistle
slide whistle
rain stick

Fabrics of all sizes

canvas
silks
cottons
ripstop nylon
bandannas
a surplus parachute

Odds and Ends

kitchen tools (pots, strainers, cups, bowls, saucepan lids, etc.)
empty cartons
cloth or paper bags
old toys (including pieces of toys)
bits and pieces of clothing
pillows
umbrellas (with blunt rather than pointy ends)

APPENDIX B
Auditions

In many cases, a director will be working with an established group that may or may not have chosen a theme, but that plans for everyone to be involved in making and performing the show.

There are cases, however, when a director will be called upon to recruit actors and/or hold auditions to form an ensemble. If there is room for only a limited number of participants in the project, casting can be tough. How to choose? Actors wanting to try out can't very well read from the script, since it hasn't yet been written. The traditional model of presenting prepared monologues may also intimidate and discourage many creative and dedicated kids who happen to have no experience in theatre.

The first step is to get prospective actors to the tryouts. An announcement in the city daily newspaper will reach a certain population: those who pay attention—or those with parents who pay attention—to the daily paper. By itself, such a notice is likely to limit the diversity of the audition pool. To expand the range of possibilities, send notices about tryouts to alternative and neighborhood newspapers, community and religious organization newsletters, schools, and radio stations. In addition to posting notices, you can make arrangements to visit community youth groups. Talk with them about the project and invite them to come. Arrange ahead of time to speak to the groups' leaders. Ask for their support in soliciting members who they feel would be good candidates for the project. To attract a cast drawn from many neighborhoods, consider holding auditions at several sites around town over the course of a few days. Many young people are much more willing to take a chance on tryouts if they can do it on their own turf. You can always work out the details of public transportation or carpooling to and from the scripting workshops, rehearsals, and performances later.

The same recruiting process can apply when working within a school. Make sure word goes out several times in the daily class announcements. Visit social studies or other classes that are discussing important social issues. Talk to those students about the project and extend a personal invitation to them to come to the tryouts. Meet with the school counselor for suggestions of likely individuals and ask the counselor to approach them first herself with the idea.

At the auditions, try to create an environment that will allow the hopefuls to shine. You are interested in learning whether they can both contribute and listen during a group discussion and, if the play's topic has been determined, what kind of passion they feel for it. If you are planning a show with music, you'll want to know about the current level of their singing or musical skills. And you'll want to see the degree to which they can think abstractly.

Meet first in a large circle to welcome everyone and describe what's about to happen. If there is more than one director or staff member working on the project, divide the crowd into smaller groups of seven or eight. Set up separate stations so that, as one group meets to talk about the project, the second group meets with another staff member to try out some theatre exercises, and, if you are planning a musical, a third group meets with the musical director to sing. After ten or fifteen minutes, each group can rotate to the next station, and after another ten or fifteen minutes, to the next. If appropriate, you can work a fourth station for movement/dance into the mix. If you are working on a smaller scale, take the entire group through each station together.

The activities in the music and discussion stations are pretty straightforward. In the former, students start by singing together and then singing individually. If you have asked them to bring an instrument, give them an opportunity to play. In the latter, they share their thoughts about the theme or about the project. At the theatre station, pattern the auditions after the exercise Investigating the Tools, described in Part One. Arrange a pile of fabrics, small musical instruments, and found objects on the floor, along with a signboard full of words from the word list that follows on p. 107. Ask the auditioners to silently choose one of the words from the list and then pick out an object or piece of fabric or instrument that will help them show what the word means. Ask each one to take a turn using one or two of the tools to explain her word to the rest as if no one else in the group understands her language. They can choose to go in any order so long as everyone gets a chance to try it. After each idea is presented, there can be a very brief opportunity for group feedback before the performer explains what her word was. Once everyone has had a turn, try another round. If there is time, they can try working in pairs. A director's assistant, taking notes on which actor did what, can be very helpful.

This approach can be much less intimidating and a lot more fun than auditions in which actors are asked to present two contrasting monologues standing alone on a stage. It also provides an opportunity for the directors to assess how each performer works with a group and whether they exhibit a gift, or even just signs of potential, for abstract thinking, a willingness to give and take in discussion, and musical ability.

Harmony

Money

Rules

Jealous

Soothing

Stuck

Support

Caught

Rights

Racism

Pain

Joy

Cheating

Disapproval

Put-Downs

Hope

Faith

Unfairness

Lonely

Loved

Intimidated

Winning

Losing

Sexism

Family

Trust

War

Fear

The World

Peace

Girls

Boys

Men

Women

Hatred

Criticism

Pride

Homesickness

Police

Taking Care

Losing a Friend

Being Honest

Hunger

America

Not Understanding

Embarrassing or Humiliating

Unwritten Rules

Friendship or Best Friends

Being Unfairly Accused

Discovering Something about Yourself

APPENDIX C
Process Checklist

Part One: Developing an Ensemble and Building Skills

The First Meeting

- ☐ Arrange seating in a circle.
- ☐ Acknowledge the participants' initiative and give them an opportunity to present themselves.
- ☐ Briefly describe the process and time line.
- ☐ Share thoughts on what the group wants from the project and how it will measure success.
- ☐ Set up promises to one another.
- ☐ Discuss respect, confidentiality, and veto power.
- ☐ Look over contracts (if appropriate).
- ☐ Spend some time doing team-building activities.

The Script Development Workshop Sessions

General Workshop Procedures

- ☐ Check-in time
- ☐ Warm-ups/tumbling
- ☐ Singing Together

Physical Confidence Exercises

- ☐ Group Juggle
- ☐ Human Knot
- ☐ Camera Above
- ☐ Sound and Movement
- ☐ Mirrors
- ☐ Counterweights
- ☐ Identify and inventory cast members' skills
- ☐ Arrange for participants to demonstrate their skills for one another (physical virtuosity)

Imagination Exercises

- ☐ Astonishing Things
- ☐ This Shows Who I Am
- ☐ Make This into Something It's Not

Investigating the Tools

Initial

- ☐ Introduce working with the tools.

Ongoing

- ☐ Investigate the tools.
- ☐ Share presentations and exchange feedback.

Part Two: Identifying and Investigating the Topic

Gathering Ideas

- ☐ Consider how to ask questions that will lead to discussions about relationships/behavior.
- ☐ Generate ideas for the Topic Cards.

Recalling Stories and Unpacking Them

Initial

- ☐ Introduce how to unpack a story; explain how to look for gests and tropes.
- ☐ Unpack a story or stories all together.

Ongoing

- ☐ Unpack stories in small groups, then gather to report on findings.

Making Connections

- ☐ Review the Unpacking Lists according to "what people did."
- ☐ Identify patterns and differences.
- ☐ Gather more imagery and text that parallels the stories.

Part Three: Building Dialogue, Lyrics, and Choreography

- ☐ Examine material in each piece for clues about what form it will take.
- ☐ Test out possibilities, fiddling with the elements developed for each: the visual and aural images, the phrases, and analogous existing material.
- ☐ Consider song lyrics; a scene; choreography; a spoken chorus; dialogue; monologues.
- ☐ Try rearranging what's familiar in a well-known story or characters.
- ☐ Try incorporating what's familiar in a well-known story or set of characters.
- ☐ Look for an ideal story that already exists.
- ☐ Present the results of first drafts and review for accuracy and for what's missing. Revise.
- ☐ To extend a piece, consider what leads up to it and what comes after. Extrapolate phrases.
- ☐ Clarify the turning points and the beginnings, middles, and endings of each piece.
- ☐ As part of the staging, remember to incorporate the tools.
- ☐ Fill out the characters with all their complexities.
- ☐ Consider using bisociation in a piece.
- ☐ Make the pieces fun to watch!

Part Four: Weaving Individual Performance Pieces into a Show

- ☐ Review the pieces created so far; make abbreviated descriptions on cards.
- ☐ Brainstorm ways to organize the pieces: a progression of episodes; place; prop; single metaphoric image; narrative; music-inspired; or some other unifying structure.
- ☐ Sketch out storyboards to test ideas.
- ☐ Separate the pieces into beginnings, middles, and endings or by contrasts.
- ☐ Consider contenders among existing pieces for openings, first act endings, and finales. If none are evident, invent some!

Part Five: Rehearsing and Performing

Preparing for Rehearsals

- ☐ Patch together pages into a manageable script.
- ☐ Complete music compositions/sheet music.
- ☐ Confirm permissions have been granted, if appropriate.
- ☐ Invite actors to cast the show or make their casting wish lists for pieces/roles.
- ☐ Cast show.
- ☐ Identify working units in script and plan rehearsal schedule.
- ☐ Move ahead with technical and promotional needs.

Rehearsals

- ☐ Meet for first read-through.
- ☐ Introduce the concept of acting as demonstrating and the value of identifying actable verbs.
- ☐ Introduce the thumb trick.
- ☐ Insist that the actors make specific choices of verbs and placement of gests.
- ☐ Offer feedback on ways to upgrade verb choices and to find the love.
- ☐ Consider ways to integrate verfremdungseffekts into the staging.
- ☐ Tighten up segues and contrasts from scene to scene.
- ☐ Progress from rehearsing the small working units to larger sections to complete run-throughs.

Performances

- ☐ Establish preshow physical and vocal warm-ups.
- ☐ Dedicate each performance.
- ☐ Check in with one another.
- ☐ Consider possibilities for postperformance follow-ups.
- ☐ Meet for closure.

APPENDIX D
Resources

TEAM-BUILDING ACTIVITIES

Participating in Challenge Courses and Ropes Courses

In Part One, I described the benefits of making arrangements for the group to start off the project by participating in a challenge course or ropes course. These are full- or half-day sessions led by trained facilitators who take groups through a series of (usually outdoor) hands-on problem-solving exercises. The exercises are all designed to inspire a team effort and to build understanding of how to work collaboratively. An excellent free resource for inquiring about availability of these programs is The Outdoor Network in Boulder, Colorado. You may contact this organization through its toll-free telephone number or its Website and the staff will do their best to put you in touch with professional facilitators in your area.

The Outdoor Network
PO Box 1928
Boulder, CO 80306–1928
USA
Tel: (800) 688-6387
E-mail: editor@outdoornetwork.com
Website: *http://www.outdoornetwork.com*

Becoming Your Own Facilitator

There is plenty of material available on the subject of learning to facilitate games and activities to build trust and cooperation. An Internet or library search for *cooperative games, experiential education, adventure education,* and *new games* will yield many possibilities.

Given limited space, I will list here some of the books that have come out of the work of Project Adventure, the organization that set the standard in this field. Its goals, and the basis of its teaching philosophy, have been summarized as follows: (1) to increase the participant's sense of personal confidence, (2) to increase mutual support within a group, (3) to develop an increased level of agility and physical coordination, (4) to develop an increased joy in one's physical self and in being with others, and (5) to develop an increased familiarity and identification with the natural world.

The following books may be useful for those who want to integrate these activities into their own work.

- Karl Rohnke, 1989, *Cowstails and Cobras II: A Guide to Games, Initiatives, Ropes Courses, & Adventure Curriculum* (Dubuque, IA: Project Adventure, Inc. in cooperation with Kendall/Hunt Publishing Company). This is a substantially revised and updated version of Project Adventure's original teaching manual (now out of print). This book offers a good selection of warm-up activities and games along with discussion of leadership issues, debriefing, and the philosophy of adventure education. It also features instructions for leading participants through various elements of a ropes course and presents a series of sample curriculum models.
- Karl Rohnke, 1984, *Silver Bullets: A Guide to Initiative Problems, Adventure Games, Stunts, and Trust Activities* (Hamilton, MA: Project Adventure, Inc.). *Silver Bullets* is a basic, very accessible collection of 165 activities, illustrated with photographs and cartoons. The book is organized into chapters covering games, stunts, initiative problems, and trust activities. Symbols identify whether the activities are designed for indoors, outdoors, or either, involve high or low activity; or require props. *Silver Bullets* is used by a variety of teachers, counselors, therapists, camp personnel, church leaders, and others.
- Karl Rohnke and Steve Butler, 1995, *Quicksilver: Adventure Games, Initiative Problems, Trust Activities, and a Guide to Effective Leadership* (Dubuque, IA: Kendall/Hunt Publishing Company). Although it is the most expensive book on the list, the outstanding thing about this one is the amount of space devoted to explaining how to be an effective group facilitator. I know of no other book that is so full of such good, practical information on the subject. Like *Silver Bullets*, the activities are numerous, well-organized, well-illustrated, and coded by symbols.
- Karl Rohnke and Jim Grout, 1998, *Back Pocket Adventure* (Needham Heights, MA: Project Adventure, Inc., published in conjunction with Simon and Schuster Custom Publishing). This slim volume, just over one hundred pages, is indeed small enough to fit into a back pocket. The idea for the book originated after Rohnke and his coauthor/colleague Jim Grout each found himself about to lead a workshop only to discover that his bag of props was lost or stolen or had strayed. Both men improvised as best they could and soon after collaborated on this compilation of activities, all of which specifically require no props. It is a very handy, simple little book.
- *Youth Leadership in Action: A Guide to Cooperative Games and Group Activities Written by and for Youth Leaders*, 1995, (Dubuque, IA: Kendall/

Hunt Publishing Company). Although the material in this book is similar to other Project Adventure guides, it offers a unique perspective. As the title implies, it was written by young people to help other youth leaders facilitate programs with peers.

Another helpful source is:

- Augusto Boal, 1992, *Games for Actors and Non-Actors*, trans. by Adrian Jackson (London: Routledge). Boal laid the foundations for his work in his seminal 1979 book *Theatre of the Oppressed*, trans. by Charles A. and Maria-Odilia Leal McBride (New York: Urizen Books). He has since written several others including this very accessible book, which includes many anecdotal illustrations of his work and a fine collection of theatre exercises.

WARM-UPS

- Bob Anderson, 1975, *Stretching* (Shelter Publications, PO Box 279, Bolinas CA 94924). This very popular book on warm-up techniques was substantially revised and re-issued in July, 2000. There are also lots of contemporary books available on yoga that will provide an excellent source for warm-ups.

SINGING

- Nick Page, 1995, *Sing and Shine On! The Teacher's Guide to Multicultural Song Leading* (Portsmouth, NH: Heinemann).
- Peter Blood and Annie Patterson, eds., 1988, *Rise Up Singing: The Group Singing Song Book* (Bethlehem, PA: Sing Out Corporation).
- Sing Out has also produced a series of audiocassettes called the *Rise Up Singing Teaching Tapes*. Six cassettes feature simple vocal and guitar renditions of all the songs in the book in the same order that they appear there. They are organized thematically according to chapter: 231 songs for children; 164 songs on community and change; 197 songs of faith; 216 (mostly) traditional folksongs; 182 songs about living and struggle; 204 songs about love and imagination. The tapes do not include the complete songs, but rather just the first verse and chorus of each, or enough of the song to learn its melody and meter.

YOUNG ACTORS' FORUM

Think globally — ACT locally!

Participant Contract

Young Actors' Forum is a non-profit theater company for youth. Its goal is to provide an opportunity for young people (ages 8-18), to collaboratively create high-quality theater works that reflect their perspectives about local and global issues. Participants develop a script together, rehearse it with support from professional directors and designers, and perform it in a professional theater setting. This production will include 40 hours of script development workshops weekdays during July and August; 35 hours of rehearsals weekday evenings and Saturdays during September, and approximately 20 hours of performances weekend evenings during September and October. The schedule is as follows:

- **Challenge course team-building day**: Saturday, July 13, 10 am -- 4 pm
- **Script Development workshops**: Monday - Thursday, 9:30 am - 2:30 pm for 4 weeks, July 15 -- August 8
- **Two-week break**: Friday, August 9 -- Sunday, August 25
- **Rehearsals**: Monday - Thursday August 26 - 29, 9:30 am to 2:30 pm
- **Evening rehearsals**: 5:45 - 8 pm 3 to 4 evenings/week & Saturdays during the first 3 weeks of September
- **Performances**: for 3 weekends, Friday/Saturday evenings, Sunday afternoons starting September 20

I, (print name) ______________________ agree to the following conditions:

I understand that this project is providing an educational opportunity and that I will receive no stipend, wages or compensation for my time nor for any material written or recorded as a result of my participation in the project.

- I will be on time to script workshops, rehearsals, and performances.
- I will be responsible for my own transportation (rides and car pools may be available).
- I will maintain the confidentiality of the group.
- I will not use or be under the influence of drugs or alcohol at the workshops, rehearsals, or performances.

I understand that grounds for possible dismissal are:

- not calling to inform the director that I will be late or absent
- more than two excused absences or tardies at the script workshops. Attendance at all rehearsals and performances is mandatory.
- breaking the confidentiality of the group
- being disruptive

______________________ signature of participant

______________ date

I, the parent/guardian of (participant's name)______________________, give my permission for her/him to participate in this project and I agree to assume any risks and hazards in connection therewith. I release Young Actors' Forum from any liability for injury or damage that may occur to (participant's name) ______________, to any other person, or to property as a result of his/her participation in this project.

______________________ signature of parent/guardian

______________ date

address: ______________________ telephone: ______________________

In case of emergency contact: ______________________ telephone: ______________________

Relationship to participant: ______________________

APPENDIX E
Elements of a Contract

In Part One I noted that a participant contract can be very useful. In addition to clarifying specific expectations, it allows the families of cast members to learn up front about the project and about the amount of time it will involve. It gives them the opportunity literally and figuratively to sign on to the project with their support. A written contract also reinforces a sense of exclusivity about the project. It sends a signal to cast members and their families that this project is a serious endeavor.

If you choose to employ a participant contract, consider including the following elements:

- a description of the purpose of the project
- the approximate amount of time that participation in the project will involve (how many hours of script development, rehearsals and performances), plus a schedule with dates, times, and locations
- a list of the house rules, or promises to one another, that the group has already agreed to follow, and a clear description of the agreed upon consequences if the conditions are not met
- a place for both the participant and parent/guardian to sign and date, as well as a place to write their home address and telephone number
- a place to write the name and telephone number of an emergency contact person for the participant

Our theatre company, Young Actors' Forum, also includes the following two clauses:

- I understand that this project is providing an educational opportunity and that I will receive no stipend, wages, or compensation for my time nor for any material written and recorded as a result of my participation in the project.

- I, the parent/guardian of (participant's name) ___________________, give my permission for her/him to participate in this project and I agree to assume any risks and hazards in connection therewith. I release the sponsors from any liability or damage that may occur to (participant's name) __________________, to any other person, or to property as a result of his/her participation in this project.

(The sponsoring organization should keep in mind that a liability release form such as this should not be used as a substitute for making sure the participant's activities are covered by some kind of liability insurance.)

NOTES

PART ONE

[1]See Don Koberg and Jim Bagnall, 1972, *The Universal Traveler: A Soft-Systems Guide to: Creativity, Problem-Solving and the Process of Reaching Goals* (Los Altos: William Kaufmann). "People become more and more creative by simply becoming more conscious of what it is they do and how what they do relates to what is in their environment" (10).

[2]Eugenio Barba and Nicola Savarese, 1991, *A Dictionary of Theatre Anthropology: The Secret Life of the Performer* (London: Routledge, 252).

[3]These exercises are borrowed and adapted from activities/games that have been around for a long time. They have been variously attributed to Viola Spolin, Karl Rohnke, who freely admits that they've been passed along to him, and others.

[4]The idea of explaining this concept with a glass of water comes from Carlo Mazzone-Clementi, a master teacher of Italian commedia dell'arte.

PART TWO

[5]For an excellent practical book on asking questions, see Norah Morgan and Julianna Saxton, 1994, *Asking Better Questions: Models, Techniques and Classroom Activities for Engaging Students in Learning* (Markham, ONT: Pembroke Publishers).

[6]These two illustrations were borrowed from Brecht's (1965) lively exposition about theatrical theory, *The Messingkauf Dialogues*, (trans. by John Willett. London: Eyre Methuen, 72). "It was like a great collection of gestures, observed with artistry. . . ; the hand that flies to one's own mouth when one is about to say too much, and the hand that falls on the wanted man's shoulder . . ."

[7]John Willet, the noted English language translator and editor of Brecht's work, had a difficult time translating the German word *gestus*. There is no contemporary English equivalent. Rather than just leave it in German, he chose to employ the obsolete English word *gest* and its adjective *gestic*, which meant "bearing, carriage, or mien."

Some Brechtian scholars prefer simply to use the German term. I have found *gest* to be very useful in explaining the sense of the term to actors because, as described in Part Two, *gest* in English works as a portmanteau word combining the words *gist* and *gesture*. See John Willett, trans. and ed., 1964, *Brecht on Theatre: The Development of an Aesthetic* (London: Eyre Methuen, 42, editor's note).

[8]See Willett, p. 105. In Brecht's words: "a gest of pain, as long as it is kept so abstract and generalized that it does not rise above a purely animal category, is not yet a social one." He further illustrates his explanation: "The pomp of the Fascists, taken at its face value, has a hollow gest, the gest of mere pomp, a featureless phenomenon: men strutting instead of walking, a certain stiffness, a lot of colour, self-conscious sticking out of chests, etc. All this could be the gest of some popular festivity, quite harmless . . . Only when the strutting takes place over corpses do we get the social gest of Fascism." (Translated by John Willett.)

This sense of the social gest is related to the second way in which Brecht made use of the term *gestus*. Along with the telling words and actions that sum up an experience, he used gestus also to describe the overall attitude of the performer toward the role. Basically, it meant that the actor put *everything* the character did into a social context. Each of those individual gests were an integral part of the big picture. They all were elements of the actor's larger gest toward the role itself. The actor shaped the individual gests so that everything the character did would reveal to the audience his attitude about that character's social motives.

[9]Strictly speaking, *trope* is a linguistic term, not a theatrical one, but, more than any other English word, it describes the intent of this exercise. In *From Archetype to Zeitgeist*, Herbert Kohl's useful book of important word definitions, the author notes that *trope* is derived not only from the Greek *trepein*, to turn away from something, but has also been linked to the Hittite *teripp*, "which also means turning but has the sense of turning over the soil, plowing it up. A trope is a turning away from the ordinary usages of language, a digging into linguistic soil to make the language more rich and fertile." In this sense, that is just what this exercise seeks to do. See Herbert Kohl et al., 1992, *From Archetype to Zeitgeist: Powerful Ideas for Powerful Thinking* (Boston: Back Bay Books, 40–41).

[10]See Vladimir Propp, 1968, *Morphology of the Folktale*, trans. by Lawrence Scott with an introduction by Svatava Pirkova-Jakobson [second edition revised and edited with a preface by Louis A. Wagner and new introduction by Alan Dundes] (Austin: University of Texas Press). "Tales were commonly lumped together . . ." (7); ". . . a tale in which a dragon counsels a young prince . . ." (88).

PART THREE

[11]The play was *Nightwalk* in Karen Malpede, ed., 1974, *Three Works by the Open Theater: Terminal, The Mutation Show, Nightwalk* (New York: Drama Books Specialists/ Publishers).

[12]In a one-man show given in Minneapolis in 1983, performance artist Chris Sullivan brilliantly integrated the story of "The Three Billy Goats Gruff" into a script about a relationship between two brothers. That performance inspired this illustra-

tion as well as the illustration of the single actor taking both parts of an interrogation scene, described in Part Five.

[13]Rebecca Rice, 1990, "Losing Faith (or Gaining Perspective)," in *Reimaging America: The Arts of Social Change* (Philadelphia and Santa Cruz: New Society Publishers, 210–11).

[14]John Fuegi, 1987, *Bertolt Brecht: Chaos According to Plan* (Cambridge: Cambridge University Press, 158).

[15]See Fuegi, 157–58.

[16]Arthur Koestler, 1964, *The Act of Creation* (New York: Dell, 35).

PART FOUR

[17]See Betty Comden and Adolph Green, 1972, Introduction to *Singin' in the Rain* (New York: Viking Press).

[18]Jim Cartwright, 1986, *Road* (London: Methuen, 1).

[19]See Ron Jenkins, 1988, *Acrobats of the Soul: Comedy and Virtuosity in Contemporary American Theatre* (New York: Theatre Communications Group, 144).

[20]Eileen Blumenthal, 1984, *Joseph Chaikin: Exploring at the Boundaries of Theater*, Directors in Perspective Series (Cambridge: Cambridge University Press, 47–48). For a fascinating look at Chaikin's work and musical structures, see Erlene Laney Hendrix, 1977, "The Presence of the Actor as Kinetic Melody: A Study of Joseph Chaikin's Open Theater Through the Philosophy of Maurice Merleau-Ponty" (Ph.D. Diss., University of Missouri–Columbia). Cited in Blumenthal.

[21]A member of the acting ensemble, quoted in A. C. H. Smith, 1972, *Orghast at Persepolis, an Account of the Experiment in Theatre Directed by Peter Brook and Written by Ted Hughes* (London: Eyre Methuen, 162).

[22]Enrique Vargas, quoted in John Lahr, 1970, *Up Against the Fourth Wall: Essays on Modern Theater* (New York: Grove Press, 47).

PART FIVE

[23]William Ball, 1984, *A Sense of Direction: Some Observations on the Art of Directing* (New York: Drama Book Publishers).

[24]Michael Shurtleff, 1978, *Audition: Everything an Actor Needs to Know to Get the Part* (New York: Walker, 29).

[25]This technique is related to something Brecht described as "fixing the not . . . but." If a character behaves in a certain way, the actors don't take it for granted that it's just the way he is. They are asked to consider what alternative behavior he's chosen not to do. The actors isolate what they believe contributes to a character or a situation

veering *not* one way *but* another. And in the way they deliver their lines, pause, and move, they make those moments clear for the audience. See Willett, p. 137.

[26]See Willett, p. 121–28.

[27]This illustration is borrowed not from Brecht, but from the Russian director Vsevolod Meyerhold. Meyerhold, one of Stanislavski's star actors, broke away from his famous mentor to find his own way, which included the use of very physical theatre to reveal social relationships. His 1922 production, *The Death of Tarelkin*, featured the title character, a petty bureaucrat, as a jester/acrobat who escaped the police on a trapeze. See Robert Leach, 1980, *Directors in Perspective: Vsevolod Meyerhold* (Cambridge: Cambridge University Press, 74).

[28]This illustration is drawn from Brecht's *The Threepenny Opera*.

[29]Transcribed from a 1991 lecture by Juan Williams at Reed College in Portland, Oregon. Used with permission in *Turn Loose the Voices*, produced by Young Actors' Forum, 1991.

[30]Ibid.

[31]See Willett, p. 83.

[32]See Fuegi, p. 34.

[33]See Alexander Dean and Lawrence Carra, 1974, *Fundamentals of Play Directing* (New York: Holt, Rinehart, and Winston).

[34]See Joseph Chaikin, 1972, *The Presence of the Actor* (New York: Atheneum, 144).

[35]Ruthanne Kurth-Schai, 1988, "The Roles of Youth in Society: A Reconceptualization," *Educational Forum* (52(2): 131–32). Quoted in Bonnie Benard, 1991, *Fostering Resiliency in Kids: Protective Factors in the Family, School, and Community* (Portland, OR: Western Regional Center for Drug-Free Schools and Communities, Northwest Regional Educational Laboratory).